*The
Courage
to Love*

The
Courage
to Love

WILLIAM SLOANE COFFIN

Harper & Row, Publishers, San Francisco
Cambridge, Hagerstown, New York, Philadelphia
1817 *London, Mexico City, São Paulo, Sydney*

Acknowledgment is made for the permission of Macmillan Publishing Co., Inc., to reprint several lines from "The Stare's Nest by My Window" from *The Collected Poems of William Butler Yeats,* copyright 1928 by Macmillan Publishing Co., Inc., renewed 1956 by Georgie Yeats.

Chapters 5 and 6 originally appeared in a somewhat different form in *Christianity and Crisis;* chapter 5 as "Homosexuality Revisited: Whose Problem?" in the November 2, 1981, issue, vol. 41, no. 17, and chapter 6 as "Abortion: Two Views—Clarity Can Be Confusing," in the October 19, 1981, issue, vol. 41, no. 16.

FIRST EDITION

Designer: Jim Mennick

Library of Congress Cataloging in Publication Data

Coffin, William Sloane.
   THE COURAGE TO LOVE.

   Contents: Introduction—The courage to love—[etc.]
   1. Sermons, American. 2. Reformed Church—Sermons.
I. Title.
BX9426.C63C68   252'.051   81-48386
ISBN 0-06-061508-7   AACR2

---

82 83 84 85 86   10 9 8 7 6 5 4 3 2 1

To my mother
CATHERINE BUTTERFIELD COFFIN
in her 90th year

Contents

Introduction

STARTING WITH the foremost of them all, Saint Paul, the Christian preachers I have most admired have sought both to engage the hearts and to inform the minds of their hearers. They have tried to link learning with love, intellect with piety, knowing that aroused but uninformed Christians are as dangerous as quack physicians. Think of the horrors associated with the Church: inquisitions and holy wars, dogmatism and ignorance, book burning, witch burning, superstition, inhibition, morbid guilt, conformity, cruelty, self-righteousness, anti-Semitism. And those horrors are not associated with the uneducated alone. As Hawthorne rightly warned, "The influential classes, and those who take upon themselves to be leaders of the people, are fully liable to all the passionate error that has ever characterized the maddest mob."

I would like to see more preachers explore the ambiguities of our time. The currents of history are churning into rapids, sweeping before them all the familiar buoys that long have marked the channels of our lives. And when we look at the ship of state, ours or almost anybody else's, all we seem to see and hear is canvas tearing and cables parting. In such disorderly and frightening times, it is no wonder that people want their answers clear, clean, and easy. But it is not the task of preachers to give their people what they want, rather, to give them what they need. And clearly what the American people do *not* need are simplistic answers that rearrange the facts of life and inevitably lead to disenchantment. For answers that begin by explaining all too much always end by explaining all too little.

The only security in life lies in embracing its insecurity. Faith in Jesus Christ, far from diminishing the risks, inspires the courage to take them on—all of them, including the risk of intellectual uncertainty.

The same holds for moral uncertainty. It is wrong for preachers to stand on every issue as if at Armageddon battling for the Lord. I know that tolerance is a tricky business often confused with indifference. But I am worried about the growing intolerance of Christians in America, about the virtue of moral indignation becoming the vice of moralism. Moralism is historically one of America's great defects. Moralism is intolerant of ambiguity; it perceives reality in extreme terms of good and evil and regards more sophisticated judgments as soft and unworthy. The temptation to moralize is strong; it is emotionally satisfying to have enemies rather than problems, to seek out culprits rather than flaws in the system. God knows it is emotionally satisfying to be righteous with that righteousness that nourishes itself on the blood of sinners. But God also knows that what is emotionally satisfying can be spiritually devastating.

That being said in support of ambiguity and uncertainty, I would like to mention two issues on which I wish more preachers would take a certain, unambiguous stand. We are living in the era of "Reaganomics," a philosophy that reverses the priorities of Mary's Magnificat by filling the rich with good things and sending the poor empty away. Reaganomics reminds me of Procrustes, the legendary Greek brigand whose habit it was to lay his victims on a bed. If they were too short, he stretched them to fit. If they were too long, he lopped off their limbs.

It occurs to me that American society—and, for that matter, the whole body of humanity—is today stretched out on an economic Procrustean bed, economics these days being the primary measure of human stature. And having been declared expendable, the marginalized millions of the world are being lopped off. Saint Paul, of course, would be appalled: "The head [cannot say] to the feet, 'I have no need of you.'" But the head is liable to say precisely that when economics run not only our banks but our hearts and minds as well.

Here at home we are having trouble balancing our budget because of our insatiable appetite for weapons. Our solution is to cut off a few more inches from society's legs—the improvident old, the unemployed young, the uninsured sick, and especially small children. The poor have become modern-day lepers. Ghettos, once a problem, are now a solution. The same is true of prisons: we put more and more people behind bars, even though that does nothing to reduce the incidence of crime.

In Old Testament times prophets spoke out when those least able to defend themselves were made to suffer most. Nations were judged by their treatment of the poor. Jesus "talked more about wealth and poverty than almost any other subject, including heaven and hell, sexual morality, the law, or violence." So I would urge my fellow clergy to plead without ceasing the cause of the oppressed. Preachers need to remind their people that "all the members of the body, though many, are one body," that to know God is to love the poor. I believe that the redistribution of wealth—at home and abroad—should be at the top of the agenda of every American church. For a more equitable distribution represents not only a measure of justice for the poor, but a measure of salvation for the rich. A second-century manual on church discipline addressed well-to-do Christians in this manner: "If you are willing to share what is everlasting, you should be that much more willing to share things which do not last."

The second item I would like to see heading every church's agenda, supported by every preacher in the land, is the goal of reversing the arms race—immediately. A. J. Musste used to say that we need a foreign policy fit for children. For their sake, and for the sake of their children, the world will need not only to be economically developed but to be disarmed as well, reorganized so that its political arrangements express the conviction that no one has anything to gain by war. Always tragic, war has become preposterous. God alone has the authority to end life on the planet—but human beings have the power. Since this power is so clearly not authorized by any tenet of the faith, I agree with the growing number of Roman Catholic bishops who assert that it is a sin to build a nuclear weapon. In repentance lies our hope—the hope that we can recognize the crisis before it is validated by disaster.

A Word on the Moral Majority

In my experience, whatever is worthy of censure is deserving as well of compassion. While I have little regard for the cause of the Moral Majority, I sympathize with American citizens who feel dispossessed by change; who feel they have lost control and power; who, as Martin Marty describes their situation, feel "left out in everyone else's liberation."

Women's, black, Chicano, gay, and other liberation movements leave them behind. The textbooks have been changed to accommodate the sensibilities of Jews, homosexuals, women, and the like. The only ethnic stereotypes one can still use and misuse are WASP, redneck, or backwoods and, to a lesser degree, Catholic ethnic. As one such WASP once told me, "In all their exoduses and liberation plots, I'm Pharaoh."

I agree with Marty's conclusion: "We will make no progress on this issue until the larger public sees the new Christian right as a tribe that feels slighted."

It is the chiefs of the tribe who trouble me most. They talk a lot—the preachers among them—of being "born again," but their reading of the third chapter of John is not the same as mine. As I understand the story, to be born again of "the spirit," as opposed to "the flesh," means to become as *vulnerable* as a child, not as innocent as a child. Holiness, not innocence, is our only option in

the sullied stream of human life. To be born again is to
see with even greater clarity the complexities of life and
our own complicity in the very evils we abhor, and to
dedicate ourselves as never before to the eradication of
these evils—even if doing so results in our being "lifted
up," as were the Son of man and many a disciple.

Continued innocence in adulthood, in contrast, seems
a deliberate denial of vulnerability. Such innocence will-
fully blinds itself to the complexities of life, which it fears
like the plague. Nor does innocence want to see, for example, our complicity as Americans in world hunger and
poverty or in the continuance of the arms race. Oddly
enough, the leaders of the Moral Majority appear to be
seeking to enter a second time into the womb to be born
of the flesh, not of the spirit. They want to be as innocent
as children in order to avoid being vulnerable as
children.

I do not mind the Moral Majority coming into the political field. The separation of church and state does not
separate a Christian from politics, and these days, Lord
knows, a faith that does not get beyond the garden gate is
a monument to irrelevance. I do object to the sins the
leaders dwell on. They are too personal, too petty. They
have little to do with the great social issues tearing our
planet apart. I object to the way the preacher-leaders put
the purity of their dogma ahead of the integrity of love.
That is not just a distortion of the Gospel; that is deser-
tion. Most of all, I object to the cause of the Moral Majority because at its core I sense the innocence of which I
have spoken. In the nuclear age, innocence should wan-
der the world wearing a leper's bell.

Throughout this volume I will insist that the opposite

of love is not hate but fear: "Perfect love casts out fear." In a funny way, fundamentalists and the military in America today share a common timidity. Both seem obsessed with creating a world in which there is nothing left to be afraid of. Amid the thorns and thistles of the wilderness, they long for Eden. But such obsessions deny dreams. If we are to broaden our vision and enlarge our hearts, we must allow risk to enter our lives, permit doubt to walk hand in hand with belief. I like what Rollo May wrote: "The most creative people neither ignore doubt nor are paralyzed by it. They explore it, admit it, and act despite it. . . . Commitment is healthiest when it is not without doubt, but in spite of doubt." I also like Rilke's words: "Be patient towards all that is unsolved in your heart and learn to love the questions themselves."

It is a mistake to sharpen our minds by narrowing them. It is a mistake to look to the Bible to close a discussion; the Bible seeks to open one. God leads with a light rein, giving us our head. Jesus told parables for this reason; stories have a way of shifting responsibility from the narrator to the hearer. Christians have to listen to the world as well as to the Word. And do not all of us learn more when we do not try to understand too soon?

I said that the Bible seeks to open a discussion. The Bible is no oracle to be consulted for specific advice on specific problems; rather, it is a wellspring of wisdom about the ambiguity, inevitability, and insolubility of the human situation. The Bible insists that each of us is a hell-deserving sinner with a sleeping hero in his or her soul. It sings praises to a God who bruises our egos but mends our hearts. The Bible shows us both the green pastures and the paths of righteousness. It talks of the greed

of the rich and the spurious omnipotence of nations.
When falsehoods weave their glittering nets around us, it
asks us to take upon ourselves the pain of truthfulness.
The Bible demonstrates that an active faith will arouse
official discontent, and it assures us of the security that
comes with the knowledge that God will ferret us out of
any hiding place: "Adam . . . where art thou?" "What
doest thou here, Elijah?" The Bible makes us comfortable
with struggle but uneasy in success.

Finally the Bible is a signpost, not a hitching post. It
points beyond itself, saying "Pay attention to God, not
me." And if, as the Bible claims, "God is love, and he
who abides in love abides in God, and God abides in
him" (or her), then revelation is in the relationship. That
is why I say the integrity of love is more important than
the purity of dogma. In all of Scripture there is no injunc-
tion more fundamental than that contained in these simple words: "Love one another."

The questions raised in this volume are important to
all of us. But I have dealt with them in sermon form hop-
ing primarily to widen and deepen the discussion of
them among my fellow Christians. In their original form
most of the sermons were heard first by my beloved parishioners, not all of whom agreed with all they heard.
But we try, parishioners and preacher alike, to remain
true to the conviction that Christian unity is based not on
agreement, but on mutual concern.

In the writing of this book I am indebted in particular
to four people: Richard Sewall, Richard Corum, Judy
Stein, and Randy Wilson.

1

The Courage

to Love

As a boy, I loved to go puddle gazing, wandering from one puddle to the next, wondering how so much of the sky could be reflected in such small bodies of water. Today I often marvel at how so much of the story of heaven and earth is captured in small biblical tales such as the story of Jesus and the paralytic. Here it is, as recorded in the second chapter of Mark:

And when he returned to Capernaum after some days, it was reported that he was at home. And many were gathered together, so that there was no longer room for them, not even about the door; and he was preaching the word to them. And they came, bringing to him a paralytic carried by four men. And when they could not get near him because of the crowd, they removed the roof above him; and when they had made an opening, they let down the pallet on which the paralytic lay. And when Jesus saw their faith, he said to the paralytic, "My son, your sins are forgiven." Now some of the scribes were sitting there, questioning in their hearts, "Why does this man speak thus? It is blasphemy! Who can forgive sins but God alone?" And immediately Jesus, perceiving in his spirit that they thus questioned within themselves, said to them, "Why do you question thus in your hearts? Which is easier, to say to the paralytic, 'Your sins are forgiven,' or to say, 'Rise, take up your pallet and walk'? But that you may know that the Son of man has authority on earth to forgive sins"—he said to the paralytic— "I say to you, rise, take up your pallet and go home." And he rose, and immediately took up the pallet and went out before them all; so that they were all amazed and glorified God, saying, "We never saw anything like this!"

Precisely what was wrong with the man neither scholars nor doctors can say. Jesus' words "My son, your sins are forgiven" indicate to us an illness related to feelings of guilt. We also suspect that at the root of every emotional disorder there is some paralyzing fear; mental wards are filled with terrified people. Like the paralytic, they are scared stiff—often in a fetal position, that being the last in which they experienced any semblance of security. And finally, we know it was widely believed in the biblical world that misdeeds caused misfortune, that sickness resulted from sin: "No ill befalls the righteous, but the wicked are filled with trouble." Alongside such pious assertions are, of course, others: "My help cometh from the Lord" (not "my ill"). Job remained skeptical of all the learned attempts to explain profound tragedy in such simplistic fashion. Wisely, we side with Job, but it would be a mistake to rule out *every* causal connection between sin and sickness. Too many of us know sicknesses—and cures—that to some mysterious degree are matters of the will. So let us assume that whatever its nature, the illness of the paralytic was, as we say, "psychosomatic."

Turning now to Jesus: to Christians he is the Incarnation, God's love in person on earth. Here again we are dealing with mystery, but what a difference there is between the love represented by Jesus and that symbolized by Cupid—an infant in diapers, blindfolded to boot! Far from blind, God's love is visionary, perceiving behind the armor most of us don almost the moment we are out of diapers an individual unprecedented and irrepeatable. And God's love doesn't seek value, it creates it. Christians recognize their value as a gift rather than an achievement: it is not because we have value that we are loved, but because we are loved that we have value. When Jesus says "My son, your sins are forgiven," his visionary love recognizes the man's need for spiritual rather than physical healing, while his creative love restores the man's worth by cleansing his heart of the fearful thoughts paralyzing his will.

I see the paralytic as a spiritual stand-in for all of us in the Christian Church whose lives—like his—have become one long suicide, whose wills—like his—are at least partially paralyzed. Whose hands are free, free to be extended to anyone? Whose feet are free to walk any path of life, free to walk out of that tight little protective circle of friends? Whose eyes are not fixed on some status symbol or other? It is inevitable: before the awesome terrors of the world every human heart quakes. Every human being tries desperately to secure himself against his insecurity—by gaining more power, more money, more virtue, more health. But the effort is vain; our need for security always outstrips our ability to provide it (a failure understood by Michelangelo, all of whose powerful figures bear the telltale sign of anxiety, dilated pupils). This anxiety is the precondition of our paralysis, which in turn produces more anxiety as we realize how we have stunted our growth, denied our destiny. Hence there is not one of us who does not need to be converted—not from life to something more than life, but from something less than life to the possibility of full life itself. "The glory of God is a human being fully alive." Irenaeus was right, and to become fully alive is undeniably possible; for to each of us, as to the paralytic, come the words "My son"—my daughter—"your sins are forgiven."

But here is where so many of us differ from the paralytic. Obviously he must have wanted to be cured as much as his four friends wanted to see him cured, because when Jesus says, "Your sins are forgiven," the paralytic believes him. When Jesus tells him to stand up, he does.

With no difficulty, I can picture myself lying on the pallet, the center of the crowd's attention. I can imagine myself enjoying the ability to use my distress to manipulate my friends. I can certainly imagine the comfort I would draw from the words "My son, your sins are forgiven." But when, following the indicative of forgiveness, I heard the imperative of responsibility—"Rise, take up your pallet, and walk"—I think my inclination would have been to murmur, "No, thanks; I think I'll just stay here on the stretcher."

What I am driving at is, I think, the central problem of the Christian Church in America today: most of us fear the cure more than the illness. Most of us prefer the plausible lie that we cannot be cured to the fantastic truth that we can be. And there is a reason: if it's hell to be guilty, it's certainly scarier to be responsible—*response-able*, able to respond to God's visionary, creative love. No longer paralyzed, our arms would be free to embrace the outcast and the enemy—the most confirmed addict, the reddest of communists. No longer paralyzed, our feet would be free to walk out of any job that is harmful to others and meaningless to us, free even to walk that lonesome valley without fear of evil. Everything is possible to those whose eyes, no longer fixed on some status symbol, are held instead by the gaze of him who is the eternal dispenser of freedom, the eternal dispenser of life.

But as the hand of love freely extended always returns covered with scars (if not nailed to a cross), it is not stupid to refuse the cure; it is not stupid to remain paralyzed, stuck on the pallet. But it is *boring.* And alas, whether they occupy pulpits or sit in pews, too many Christians are still on the pallet. Like the paralytic, they know they are sinners, at least they know in a vague sort of way. But lacking his will to be cured, lacking the courage to be well, they do not seek the forgiveness that offers a new way of life; instead they seek punishment—which, by assuaging the guilt, makes the old way of life bearable anew. They find this punishment not only in

boring sermons and services, but also in a religion of le-
galism and moralism that turns people who could be free
and loving into mean little Puritans, bluenosed busy-
bodies passing judgment on others instead of themselves
being just.

Let's switch images for a moment. Do you remember
the story of the rich young ruler who eagerly sought out
Jesus for advice, only to turn down the advice and go
sorrowfully away? I think we are like him. When, in distress, we seek guidance, we think we want to change
when actually we want to remain the same—but feel better about it. In psychological terms, we want to be more
effective neurotics, "preferring the security of known
misery to the misery of unfamiliar insecurity." But, once
again, is it not boring—this secure, paralyzed life, this deliberate retreat from the mysterious to the manageable,
from freedom to bondage? Is it not dull to live life to the
minimum, to be devout but not daring? Surely the art of
life is to die young as late as possible. Why, then, like the
paralytic before his cure, do we seek to do just the opposite? Furthermore, for Christians at least, it is dishonest to
go on living in fear and guilt as if the cure were not there
within our very reach.

It is popular these days to berate secular humanism
and atheistic communism. But the heresy of rejecting
Christ is insignificant compared to the heresy of remak-
ing Christ into something he never was, is not now, and
never will be. We cannot say that we are Christians and
then pretend that Christ is not the healer, the eternal dispenser of freedom and life. Nor can we pretend that
God's love in person on earth—the Incarnation—does not

say altogether as much about what we are to become as it does about what God has become.

The courage to be well is a crucial virtue. With the currents of history threatening to carry before them everything we have loved, trusted, looked to for pleasure and support, we are called on to live with enormous insecurity. The churches could become centers of creative and courageous thinking. They could also become sanctuaries for frightened Americans, recruiting grounds for authoritarian figures and movements, some of which already bear the earmarks of an emerging fascism.

Will we be scared to death or brought to life? It all depends on where we find our ultimate security. Will it be in our own fears and guilt or in God Almighty, of whom we have but to ask for a thimbleful of help in order to receive an oceanful?

"My son, your sins are forgiven. . . . Rise, take up your pallet, and walk." Where the man went we do not know, for Jesus healed with no strings attached. But responding, as he apparently did, to God's love with his own, we need not worry; for "eye hath not seen, nor ear heard, neither have entered into the heart of man, the things which God hath prepared for them that love him."

"The glory of God is a human being fully alive."

Suggested Reading

Sheldon Kopp, *If You Meet the Buddha on the Road, Kill Him!* (New York: Bantam, 1976).

2
The Limits
of Life

To become fully alive we have to recognize and be done with our manifold forms of paralysis. But freedom also demands our recognition that life itself has limits. "Life is limitation": it cannot be said too often. Nor can the positive side of that statement be sufficiently stressed, for just as a stream has no chance of running deep until it finds its banks, so we, until we discover our limits, have not a prayer of becoming profound.

Of all life's limitations the greatest, of course, is death. Death is an event that embraces one's entire life. "I have but one life to live" is a thought that never leaves us. But consider for a moment the alternative—endless existence. Without death, life would be interminable! I have a private nightmare: I will live for hundreds of years in an armchair hooked up to an Empire State Building of extra kidneys and hearts and livers. No, I am glad life is short.

Had we all the time in the world, we would never use any of it. We would become, in Thurber's phrase, "blobs of glub." We'd be as bored as the old Greek gods and no doubt be up to the same frivolous tricks. Moreover, for some people life is cruel; they have a right to see an end to it. And if life is good, as fundamentally it surely is, then we should be willing to get out of the way and let others have a crack at it.

I do not mean to make light of death. Whether life is good or bad, death is so awesome and terrifying that the sooner we use our faith to come to terms with it, the better off we are. But finally, death is more friend than foe.

Another kind of limitation has to do with our talents. When we are young we dream big. We are going to sing like Luciano Pavarotti, dance like Patricia McBride, write like Maya Angelou, have the courtroom career of Louis Nizer or the lashlike left of pitcher Ron Guidry. But then, say at age thirty-five, comes the cold shower, the sharp contrast between the dream and what became of it. Suddenly we realize we are not going to sing, dance, write, orate, or pitch like anyone but ourselves. It is discouraging, but also creative; it is another important crisis of faith, for the art of Christian life is to take such defeats and turn them into the occasions for the victories God always had in mind for us. It is not God who wants us to seek status; through his love He has already given us that, and to each the same. God does not want us to prove, only to express, ourselves.

What a different world we would live in were all of us to express rather than prove ourselves! Instead of slaves to status, we would be free people of the Lord. We would be like the shepherds about whom we hear so much and think so little at Christmas. It was low-down work keeping watch over those flocks by night, and no doubt a lot of people considered them low-down folk. Yet a multitude of the heavenly host appeared unto them. And consider this: after the shepherds had seen the Christ Child, did they run off and become lawyers and doctors? No, they went back to tending their sheep, which was a good thing for the sheep and for the people needing the wool. If, like the shepherds, we seek to express our talents rather than vindicate our pride, we shall find meaning in whatever we do.

There is a third kind of limitation. We want to be Pavarotti *and* McBride *and* Angelou *and* Nizer *and* Guidry. *We want it all*—just the way we did when as small children we stood for the first time in a cafeteria line; just as Adam and Eve did in the garden; just as Jesus did in the wilderness when the devil promised him the whole world for a seemingly small price.

Here is how a modern writer, Sam Keen, put the matter for himself, and for many of us.

There are so many lives I want to live, so many styles I would like to inhabit. In me sleeps Zorba's concern to allow no lonely woman to remain comfortless ("Here am I, Lord, send me!"), Camus' passion to lessen the suffering of the innocent, Hemingway's drive to live and write with lucidity, and the unheroic desire to see each day end with tranquility and a shared cup of tea.

I am so many, yet I may be only one. I mourn for all the selves I kill when I decide to be a single person. Decision is a cutting-off, a castration. I travel one path only by neglect-ing many. Actual existence is tragic, but fantastic existence (which evades choice and limitation) is pathetic. The human choice may be between tragedy and pathos, Oedipus and Willy Loman. So I turn my back on small villages I will never see, strange flesh I will never touch, ills I will never cure, and I choose to be in the world as a husband and a father, an explorer of new ideas and styles of life. Yet per-haps Zorba will not leave me altogether. I would not like to live without dancing, without unknown roads to explore, without the confidence that my actions were helpful to some.

I like that passage, and I agree with Keen that life is either tragic or pathetic. But how could it be otherwise? Choice is at the core of life. Without choice, without the hard choices Adam and Eve refused to make and Jesus accepted, life would not be human at all. Yet it is difficult to accept the notion that life is limitation. Few of us really accept death, or the limits of our talents, or the choices we have to make in order to be the best we can be. Or let us say that what we know intellectually we cannot al-ways appropriate emotionally, if only because the long-est, most arduous trip in the world is the journey from the head to the heart. But until that trip is complete we cannot be free; we remain at war with ourselves, and of course those at war with themselves are those who make casualties of others, even of friends and loved ones.

What is true of personal life is equally true of national life. Nations at war with themselves displace their vio-lence abroad in promiscuous interventions. Nations, like people, do not live forever; there are limits to their talents, and no more than individuals can they have it all. Primarily they cannot be at one and the same time the most powerful *and* the most virtuous. It is gratifying for Americans to recall that ours is the longest-lived revolution in the world, maybe even the most successful. But it would be a mistake to forget that our influence as a people was greatest when as a nation we were weakest. We rallied more hopes and energies when we had no rockets and little muscle. The other day, I shuddered to read words of Alexander Hamilton more pertinent to our time than to his: "To be more safe they [nations], at length, will eventually become more willing to run the risk of being less free." The greatness of our country has been its freedom, its ability to abide its critics, its recognition that freedom of speech is a right that must be most highly prized when its exercise is most offensive. At our best we Americans have recognized that freedom's primary defense lies in freedom's use. The danger today is that we might become more concerned with defense than with having things worth defending.

"Actual existence is tragic, but fantastic existence (which evades choice and limitation) is pathetic." On second thought, I find that statement a bit too negative. As I said at the beginning, it is a good thing that life is limitation. Without death, we would never live. Without discovering the limits of our talents, we would never discover who we are. And finally, hard choices have a potential for riches beyond reckoning. Deserted by his disciples, in agony on the cross, barely thirty years old, Christ said, "It is finished." Thus ended the most complete life ever lived.

We need not endlessly grieve the distant villages we will never see. We need not grieve the strange flesh we will never touch, the wrongs we will never right, the ills we will never cure. I'm against quietism, but I think I have lived just long enough to learn that contentment lies in discerning the value of the things we have, long enough to understand what Saint Paul meant when he wrote, "For all things are yours; whether Paul, or Apollos, or Cephas, or the world, or life, or death, or things present, or things to come; all are yours; and ye are Christ's; and Christ is God's."

3

Thorns

in the Flesh

WHILE ON the subject of limitations, we would probably do well to consider one more kind—"thorns in the flesh," in Saint Paul's metaphor. They are small things, thorns—like blips on a large screen. But as we know, a small blip can sink you.

As in Saint Paul's case, a thorn in the flesh might be a physical disability. Those of us lucky enough to have been spared bad genes or tragic accidents can never, I think, show sufficient admiration (not pity, which is mixed with condescension) for those who have been maimed physically, yet have remained intact spiritually.

But a thorn in the flesh may also be psychosomatic; Moses, it would seem, had a stammer. A thorn may be entirely psychological, like Jeremiah's overwhelming sense of his own insufficiency. Think of the thorns being borne right now, all over this country, all over the world.

Some are thorns of grief—for the pointless death of a child, a husband, a wife. Others are thorns of betrayal. One of Arthur Miller's characters in *After the Fall* says, "O God, why is betrayal the only truth that sticks?"

A thorn can also be a divorce, long past, that still poisons the bloodstream of our lives. A thorn can be a child we think has disgraced us, or one we think we have disgraced. A thorn can be any lapse of judgment or mistake. The way we treasure mistakes sometimes makes me think they are the holiest things in our past.

You see what I'm getting at: in this world there are things hoped for, and things stuck with. The thorns are what we are stuck with. We cannot extract them. All of them cause pain, the real pain that is associated with loss: loss of health; loss of faith and hope, as when we somehow feel "unblessed"; loss of joy; loss of love; and certainly loss of power. To see how pained we are by loss of power we have only to recall the thorn in the flesh of the nation represented by those fifty-three hostages we could not seem to extract from Iran. So humiliated were we as a people that today we feel compelled to turn almost any foreign affairs issue into a test of strength.

Take a moment and think of a real thorn in your own flesh, a real "messenger of Satan" in your life. Pick one, and then let's see if we can deal with our thorns the way Saint Paul dealt with his.

Perhaps you cannot think of one. Maybe you are luckier than most. More likely it is because your wounds are too deep to examine. If so, that is sad, because what is beyond recall is generally beyond redemption. Saint Paul, of course, is keenly conscious of his thorn. He tells us:

"Three times I besought the Lord about this, that it should leave me. . . ."

Generally, prayer is not an act of self-expression. Prayer is an act of empathy; prayer is thinking God's thoughts after him. Prayer is praying *"Our* father who art in heaven" when everything within us longs to cry out *"My* father," because "our" includes that horrible divorced husband, that wayward child; it includes muggers, rapists, the Iranian captors, all the people who jam thorns into our flesh.

But sometimes prayer *is* an act of self-expression. It was to Saint Paul: "Three times I besought the Lord about this, that it should leave me. . . ." When we do express our feelings to God, we should, like Paul, be as specific as possible. Do not pray, "Lord, I am in pain"; say, "Lord, feel the throbbing in my right knee," or "Lord, you know how heavy my heart is with grief since Johnny died." There is too much dignity in too many prayers—dignity at the expense of specificity. It is really a fake dignity, the kind that puts taste ahead of truth. So never mind how crude or how trivial your prayers may sound to you. There are no unimportant tears to God.

"Three times I besought the Lord . . ." What do you suppose happened the first time? What happened the second and third times? I suspect that the first time Paul probably did not receive the answer he records in the letter to the Corinthians. It would make more sense if by way of an answer he heard nothing, but rose from prayer a better person. That is no mean answer; it is, in fact, answer sufficient in many cases. In other words, the first time Paul simply unburdened himself of his anger, his grief, and his frustration. In this crazy, mixed-up world you have to "dump the mud." Do not be so proud as to think you do not have to; all of us do. I have a friend who is a monk, probably the most saintly person I know. In a recent meeting, a man was saying cruel things. Suddenly this monk got up, walked across the room, and punched him right in the nose. Even a saint has to dump the mud, although on the nose of another person is probably not as good a place as in the lap of the Almighty.

Now what about the second time? It would be true to life if the second time Paul received an answer that went something like this: "I hear what you're saying, Paul, but let me remind you that it takes both sunshine and rain to make one of my rainbows. You are a keen observer of the human condition. You know that people tend to live merely in the service of their own success. Those who know nothing but prosperity and pleasure become hard and shallow. Those whose prosperity has been mixed with adversity can be kind and gracious. And civilization, from a heavenly point of view, is only a slow process of learning to be kind."

Obviously tension is the pulse of life. As Blake said, "Without contraries is no progression." Moreover, what makes us unhappy can also make us more alive. Pain can bring more life than pleasure. But for this kind of life to sprout and flourish we have to stop denying and defying these thorns. We have to begin to accept them; we have to befriend the enemy. The Talmud says the true hero is one who makes the enemy a friend. Let us apply that insight to our own internal enemies. Each of us has a whole community of folk dwelling inside us; some are friendly, and others real enemies. When for the second time we take our thorn to the Lord, we have to allow the Lord to help us begin to embrace the thorn. In this world you have to take your whole life in your arms, and allow yourself and your life to be embraced by the almighty arms of God. That, it seems to me, would be a good agenda for the second time—to start the process of acceptance.

Then—a while later—comes the third time. My guess is that the third time, Paul discovers the true mercy of failure. "Three times I besought the Lord about this, that it should leave me; but he said to me, 'My grace is sufficient for you, for my power is made perfect in weakness.'" That is one of the great lines of Scripture, but not an easy one to understand.

I said that human beings tend to live merely in the service of their own success. And to individuals and nations alike, success tends to spell power. Then, when we seek to exert power over others, we lose it over ourselves. The reason for this seems simple: by nature most of us are neither humble nor reasonable. Freud said that intelligence is weak, if persistent. And Isaac Bashevis Singer, in accepting his Nobel Prize, pointed out that he thought the Almighty was frugal when it came to the intellect, lavish when it came to passions and emotions. Among these passions and emotions are, of course, ambition, greed, the instinct to dominate, the needs of the ego—a whole bundle of personal vanities and anxieties. Only when they are contained do reason and the Holy Spirit have a chance. That is why, I think, God's power is made perfect in weakness.

I am sure that many of you have read, "Blessed are

the meek," and wondered what that meant. Does that
mean you are supposed to become a doormat for people
to walk over? Certainly a lot of Christians act as if that is
what it meant. But the word in Greek is *praös*, and that
word, as a verb, refers to the channeling of energies, as in
taming horses. Before they could be useful, horses had to
be "meeked." In Wycliffe's Bible we read, "Blessed are
the meeked, for they shall inherit the earth."

We are meeked by the thorns in our flesh. The mercy
of our failures is that they point us toward true success,
which we have reluctantly to admit is with God alone. So
a "messenger of Satan" can become a servant of God; the
devil's subtraction can become God's addition: "When I
am weak, then I am strong."

So if you are up for it, take your Bible and read not
only the twelfth chapter of Second Corinthians, but also
the fourth chapter. Read, "But we have this treasure in
earthen vessels, to show that the transcendent power belongs to God and not to us." Read, "We are afflicted in
every way, but not crushed; perplexed, but not driven to
despair; struck down, but not destroyed; always carrying
in the body the death of Jesus, so that the life of Jesus
may also be manifested in our bodies." Then go to work.
Describe to God in minute detail just how you feel about
that thorn in your flesh. And make it sound as full of
self-pity and anger as you feel; make it sound as trivial as
you want. But make it specific; get it all out. And do not
ask for answers: "Lord, just listen to me; I don't want to
hear anything." A week later, try it again. Maybe you
will have to do it several times, if you are as angry as I
am about a couple of thorns in my own flesh. But I'll tell

you something: you get bored with your bitterness. After a while it gets dull dumping the mud ("I said that last week, Lord; I'm beginning to get tired of repeating it"). So the third time, you may find that you can begin the process of integration, begin to befriend the enemy.

Let us go back to Saint Paul: "And to keep me from being too elated . . . a thorn was given me in the flesh, a messenger of Satan, to harass me, to keep me from being too elated. Three times I besought the Lord about this, that it should leave me; but he said to me, 'My grace is sufficient for you, for my power is made perfect in weakness.'" Then with a kind of nose-thumbing independence Paul says, "I will all the more gladly boast of my weaknesses, that the power of Christ may rest upon me. For the sake of Christ, then, I am content with weaknesses, insults, hardships, persecutions, calamities. . . ." And he ends triumphantly, "For when I am weak, then I am strong."

4

Being
Called

For the most part, we have been talking of ourselves as individual human beings, which is perfectly all right as long as we remember that Christians do not believe in the cult of the individual ego. That cult is as bloody as that of the Aztecs; it feeds on victims. A modern novelist writes of "indulging in that greed for personal salvation which might be the most obnoxious greed there is."

Let us consider the call of God as it came to biblical prophets such as Isaiah and Moses. The call of Isaiah took place twenty-seven centuries ago, and Moses' even earlier. God has been calling people for a long time. Yet the meaning of a call is far from clear. Today only ministers get "called"—which leaves doctors, lawyers, merchants, artists, social workers, teachers, moms, dads, people who have made their peace with society, people who have

fled it, and still others determined to overthrow it. Has
none of them a calling? What exactly do we mean by a
call from God?

If "God is love," then in responding to God we respond also to one another, and by "one another" I do not
mean only the other members of our family, important as
they are, or that tight little circle of friends I mentioned
in the first chapter. Jesus said, "Inasmuch as ye have
done it unto one of the least of these my brethren, ye
have done it unto me." To be converted by Christ is to be
converted to the poor. Let me say explicitly what up to
now I have only implied: There is no way that Christianity can be spiritually redemptive without being socially
responsible. A Christian cannot have a personal conversion experience without experiencing at the same time a
change in social attitude. God is always trying to make
humanity more human. But without us God will not, just
as without God we cannot. So every time we lift our eyes
to heaven and cry out, "Lord, . . . how long shall the
wicked triumph? How long shall they utter and speak
hard things?" at that very moment you can be sure God
is putting precisely the same question to us. So our calling is simply to help God protect, affirm, and dignify
life—more and more of it.

To see how all this works out let us turn to the opening twelve verses of the third chapter of Exodus. Here we
read of God's well-known call—"Moses, Moses"—and of
Moses' reply, "Here am I." At the time, Moses has been
playing essentially a spectator's role. In his youth, he had
been part of what might be termed "the struggle," but
only impulsively; after killing the Egyptian guard he had

fled. Then he entered what psychologists like to call "a period of consolidation." He went to Midian, married, had a fine boy, entered his father-in-law's business; he settled down. Suddenly in the midst of all that security he hears, "Moses, Moses.... Come, I will send you"— right back into the thick of everything he had tried so hard to escape.

Let me offer a modern-day analogy. During the years I lived and worked in New Haven, Connecticut, I frequently took the train to New York City. It was easy, I noticed, to remain a spectator as I watched Fairfield and then Westchester counties go by outside the window. But then, suddenly, the train would slow and pull into the first New York stop, the 125th Street station in upper Manhattan. Now, outside the window, in place of Long Island Sound, gentle hills, and manicured lawns, I saw Harlem at its harshest—burned-out buildings and shabby signs and, on the streets, truncated, embittered human life. I found myself being pulled out of my spectator's role. I felt myself coming under some strange kind of judgment as I began to feel my own complicity in the evil I saw and abhorred. So it was a great relief when, instead of all those sad and passive or angry faces, I saw my own face reflected back, as the train—thank God!— entered the tunnel that leads to Grand Central Station.

"Then the Lord said, 'I have seen the affliction of my people who are in Egypt, and have heard their cry because of their taskmasters; I know their sufferings, and I have come down to deliver them out of the hand of the Egyptians.' "

Even in faraway Midian, Moses could not turn a totally deaf ear to the cry of his own people. (That fine boy of his he had named Gershon, which means "I live as a sojourner in a foreign land.") In other words, God's call to Moses was embedded in a cry of pain, and it was a call to alleviate that pain by sharing it.

The same is true of the calls that came to Samuel, to Elijah, to Amos, to Isaiah, to Jeremiah, to Jesus as well—Jesus, who arose that day in the synagogue to read from Isaiah, "He has sent me to proclaim release to the captives and recovering of sight to the blind."

Jesus delivered people from paralysis, insanity, leprosy, suppurating wounds, deformity, and muteness. But again and again in word and deed he returned to the plight of the poor—whose poverty, in true prophetic fashion, he considered no historical accident but the fruit of social injustice. What would he say and do in our hard and uncertain times, in a world one-half of whose children never so much as open their mouths to say "aah" to a doctor, a world in which almost every country is robbing the poor to feed the military? And would he not pronounce our own nation a greedy disgrace? Whole cities could live on the garbage from our dumps, in the clothes we wear but once, on the luxuries we consider necessities. The world with its triumphs and despairs, its beauty and ugliness, has today moved next door to every one of us. Only spiritual deafness can prevent our hearing the voice of God in the clamor of the cities. Only blindness of a willful sort can prevent our seeing the face of Christ in the faces of the suffering poor.

But let us not—once again—be paralyzed by guilt. To our comfort let us recall that when Moses first received

his marching orders he was not happy. Far from falling
on his knees, he reared up on his hind legs: "Who am I
that I should go to Pharaoh, and bring the sons [and
daughters] of Israel out of Egypt?"

How I love that cry of protest! We forget that a relationship that makes no room for anguished argument
leaves little room for honesty either, that premature sub-
mission is but a facade for repressed rebellion—which
may be why so many Christians are so hostile!

And Moses was not the only prophet initially to resist. "Ah, Lord God!" said Jeremiah, "Behold, I do not
know how to speak, for I am only a youth"—words a
modern prophet might well have repeated, for Martin
Luther King was all of twenty-seven when in the front of
that Montgomery, Alabama, bus in 1957 "Rosa Parks sat
down and all the world stood up."

But if there are reasons to resist the call of God, there
are stronger ones to accept. In answer to Moses' objec-
tions, God says, "But I will be with you." Let me ask you:
Could God have been with Moses in the same way had
Moses elected to stay in Midian? For that matter, could
Moses have become Moses? Jeremiah, Jeremiah? The
Good Samaritan, the Good Samaritan? Just as the call of
God is embedded in a cry of pain, so the acceptance of
God's call is at one with our self-fulfillment. We give,
true, but in return we receive so much—our whole iden-
tity. "Cogito, ergo sum," said Descartes: "I think, therefore I am." Nonsense! *Amo,* ergo sum—I love, therefore I
am. In these hard and uncertain times, in a world so full,
as always, of busy sinners and lazy saints, we are as we
love. Love is the name of our journey. It is love that mea-

sures our stature. There is no smaller package in all the world than that of a person all wrapped up in himself. Deny it, stifle it, still it lives, this love, in each and every one of us, as a tiny spark that will not die—although of course it tortures terribly, because all the odds are against its continued burning.

And we can go further: *We* love, therefore we are the Church. Think back to the story of the paralytic: four friends—who moreover remain nameless—carry a fifth, desperately ill, to the fount of all healing. What a symbol of the Church at her best! If Christ is God's love personified, the Church is God's love organized.

Essentially every church, every personal vocation represents love in search of form. As I read the lives of the Berrigan brothers, the message is not that everyone should do as they do, although Lord knows there is much to recommend civil disobedience as the best answer to the mad momentum of the arms race. The more enduring message is that we should not make our peace with the world as it is, but rather move to the creative edge of whatever estate we happen to occupy. I know, for example, of community organizers, politicians, cops too, in wretched neighborhoods of New York who are viewed by the inhabitants as bright lights in their dark streets. I know of a church in a rundown part of Philadelphia that has organized a community bank and bought a radio station to be a voice for the voiceless. I know businesspeople whose money speaks, proclaiming literally the recovery of sight to the blind. And always these churches and these individuals champion justice, seeking not only to alleviate the results of poverty, but more importantly, to eliminate its causes.

What is worth living for is also worth dying for. Moses knew he would be lucky to get out of Egypt alive. Martin Luther King was not lucky. And neither, more recently, was Archbishop Romero of El Salvador, who in a nationwide broadcast took on the junta of his long-suffering country: "I implore you, I beg of you, nay, I order you, in the name of God, stop the repression!" Within a week he was shot dead in a church. It is sad, terribly sad, when a good person dies, but is it tragic when people do not count their own lives dear and lay them down for their friends? "By this we know love, that he laid down his life for us; and we ought to lay down our lives for the brethren" (and sisters). Death is the meeting place of all that lives, and whereas a natural death changes only the self, a martyr dies to change the world. The cross of Christ is more a symbol of life than of death, for it takes a lot of living to be selected as a target for martyrdom.

"Moses, Moses" ... "Mary" ... "John" ... "Our Lady of Sorrows" ... "First Presbyterian" ... "Second Baptist." Fill in your own name and church. There is no question that the air is full of calls, for the city, the nation, the world is full of pain. The only question is which of us, and which of our churches (after some stout resistance) will find the courage, imagination, and grace to reply, "Here am I" ... "Here are we."

Suggested Reading

Jim Wallis, *The Call to Conversion* (San Francisco: Harper & Row, 1981).

5

Homosexuality

ASIDE FROM their extraordinary contributions to
human progress and happiness, what did the following
have in common: Erasmus, Leonardo da Vinci, Michelangelo, Christopher Marlowe, King James I of England, Sir
Francis Bacon, Thomas Gray, Frederick the Great of Ger-
many, Margaret Fuller, Tchaikovsky, Nijinsky, Proust, A.
E. Housman, T. E. Lawrence, Walt Whitman, Henry
James, Edith Hamilton, W. H. Auden, Willa Cather, and
Bill Tilden, the greatest tennis player of his time?

Some of you, no doubt, have the answer: they were
all homosexual. And why do I bring up this subject,
probably the most divisive issue since slavery split the
Church? Because the once unmentionable has become
unavoidable. Christian ministers are claiming divine authority for the judgment that gay men and women are
not only different, but sinfully different; gay men and
women are being physically and psychologically abused;
they are being excluded from their families, frozen out of

churches, and discriminated against in a variety of pain-
ful legal ways. We have no choice but to bring up the
issue. Straight and gay American citizens, and especially
American Christians, can remain neither indifferent nor
indecisive.

What is hard, of course—and hard for many gays
too—is to approach the subject with open minds rather
than fixed certainties, with hearts full of compassion
rather than repugnance. That is why I suggest you read
the biblical account of Saint Peter's struggle to abandon
his own fixed certainties, to overcome his own repugnance. In Acts 10:1–20 he protests three times when in
his trance he hears the Lord order him to rise and kill
and eat birds and reptiles and pigs. Hardly surprising,
when you remember that ever since he was a tot he has
had it drilled into him: "Every swarming thing that
swarms upon the earth is an abomination; it shall not be
eaten. Whatever goes on its belly, and whatever goes on
all fours, or whatever has many feet, all the swarming
things that swarm upon the earth, you shall not eat; for
they are an abomination." That is Holy Writ, part of the
holy Levitical Code, the Word of God as Jews understood
it. And now God suddenly is telling Peter just the opposite: "Kill and eat. . . . What God has cleansed, you must
not call common." Moreover, all his life Peter has been
instructed not to associate with Gentiles. But when the
emissaries of Cornelius arrive, Peter accompanies them to
the latter's house, where Peter confesses, "Truly I perceive that God shows no partiality, but in every nation
any one who fears him and does what is right is acceptable to him."

So the question is whether those of us who were

drilled, as was Peter, to think a certain way are as willing
as he to risk reexamining what we were taught. Moral
judgment has a progressive character, criticizing the present in terms of the future. Perhaps the Holy Spirit in our
time is leading each of us to a new conviction, a new
confession: "Truly I perceive that God shows no partiality, but *in every sexual orientation* any one who fears him
and does what is right is acceptable to him."

Several years ago James B. Nelson, a professor of
Christian ethics, suggested that there were four primary
theological stances toward homosexuality. The first was a
rejecting-punitive position; the second a rejecting-non-
punitive position; the third a conditional acceptance; and
the fourth an unconditional acceptance. I think these four
positions reflect the differing attitudes of most church
members today.

The Jerry Falwells of the land obviously take the rejecting-punitive position. To them homosexual acts are
perverse, repugnant, and sinful. Like Peter's argument
with God, theirs too is based on Levitical law—in this
case, "You shall not lie with a male as with a woman; it is
an abomination."

What they never point out is that "abomination" (*toe-
vah* in Hebrew)—the word used in reference to homosexual acts—is also used in reference to eating pork, to misuse of incense, and to intercourse during menstruation.
Generally it does not signify something intrinsically evil
(like rape or theft, which are also dealt with in the Levitical Code), but something that is ritually unclean. So, like
Peter, we may be called to recognize the distinction between intrinsic wrong and ritual impurity.

There are some other things never mentioned by the

Jerry Falwells. To avoid idolatry, the Israelites went to great lengths to separate their worship of God from the fertility cults of their neighbors, whose rituals involved male as well as female prostitutes. But their primary concern was with idolatry, not homosexuality. Likewise they rejected the practice widespread in the Middle East at the time of humiliating captured foes by forcing them to submit to anal rape in a fashion similar to what goes on in prisons today. Again, the emphasis was not on prohibiting homosexuality; it was on not dishonoring a fellow human being. It was also widely believed—and by the Israelites as well in this case—that the male seed alone carried life; women provided only the incubating space. Hence any ejaculation outside of a woman's body was a form of abortion, and procreation was mighty important to a very small nation in a sea of hostile ones.

Most of all, what we need to remember is that nowhere does Scripture address a specifically homosexual orientation. Biblical writers assume that homosexual acts are being committed by people whose basic orientation is heterosexual. The problem they are addressing is, in modern terms, perversion rather than inversion. The Bible says nothing directly one way or another about the loving, lasting relationships known by so many of the people I listed at the outset, the loving, lasting relationships that patently exist today between so many gay people in this country, in every city, and in so many churches.

As for Sodom and Gomorrah, scholars are far less clear about what happened there than are most contemporary evangelists. If, however, we allow the Bible to illumine its own cloudy passages, we find that the destruction of Sodom and Gomorrah had little if anything to do with homosexuality. In Ezekiel we read, "This was the guilt of your sister Sodom: she and her daughters had pride, surfeit of food, and prosperous ease, but did not aid the poor and needy." In the first chapter of Isaiah, where Judah is rebuked through a comparison with Sodom, homosexuality is never mentioned among the specific sins, which again include a failure to pursue justice and to champion the oppressed. The most likely other sin of Sodom was a failure to show hospitality to strangers—a possibility indicated by Jesus' words to his disciples: "Whenever you enter a town and they do not receive you . . . I tell you it shall be more tolerable on that day for Sodom than for that town." How ironic that because of a mistaken understanding of the crime of Sodom and Gomorrah, Christians should be repeating the *real* crime every day against homosexuals!

Clearly, it is not Scripture that creates hostility to homosexuality, but rather hostility to homosexuality that prompts certain Christians to retain a few passages from an otherwise discarded law code. The problem is not how to reconcile homosexuality with scriptural passages that appear to condemn it, but rather how to reconcile the rejection and punishment of homosexuals with the love of Christ. I do not think it can be done. I do not see how Christians can define and then exclude people on the basis of sexual orientation alone—not if the law of love is more important than the laws of biology.

The rejecting but nonpunitive stance, while condemning homosexual acts, strives not to condemn the homosexual person. According to this second view, homosexuals are not criminals or sinners so much as victims of arrested development or some other form of psychic disorder, because fundamentally homosexuality is "unnatural." The problem with this position is that most gay people assert that they did not choose their orientation, they discovered it; and scientific research supports the assertion. Psychology professor John Money, a leading authority on character development, claims that it is not possible to force a change from homosexual to heterosexual "any more than it is possible to change a heterosexual into a homosexual." If that is the case, the offer to "cure" gays of their "sickness" carries the danger of raising false expectations, and then guilt when the cure does not work. Besides, how sick are gays? I was impressed when in 1973 the American Psychiatric Association voted to remove homosexuality from its list of mental disorders. The association did not deny that many homosexuals are disturbed, it only acknowledged that many are not. And what is the meaning of "natural" and "unnatural"? I come back to the law of love and the laws of biology. If we as Christians judge what is natural according to the law of love, and if we can affirm that gays can be as loving as straights, then why is homosexual love contrary to human nature? Should a relationship not be judged by its inner worth rather than by its outer appearance?

That brings us to the stance of conditional acceptance. Many sensitive straight Christians have struggled to reach this position. They now believe that all rights should be accorded gay people. They believe in the ordination of avowed gays, if only because they see the hypocrisy involved in supporting job opportunities outside the church only to deny these same opportunities within. But they cannot picture a gay spouse in the parsonage; they are uncomfortable with public displays of gay affection. In their heart of hearts they feel that homosexuality is not really on a par with heterosexuality.

I have tended to lean toward that position, but I think it is untenable. Consider Jewish-Christian relations. Most Christians will insist that Jews should enjoy the same rights as Christians because they are as good or as bad as we are; we are all equal. Nevertheless in their heart of hearts they think Judaism is inferior to Christianity. But can you champion equality while nourishing the theological roots that make for inequality? Finally, does not Judaism have to be not inferior, not superior, just different? There are dilemmas, major ones, particularly for Christians who feel that Jews never recognized God's love in person on earth. But dilemmas we can live with and even find creative; the worst thing we can do with a dilemma is to resolve it prematurely because we lack the courage to live with uncertainty.

I think straight Christians have to reach the same position vis-à-vis gays. They are different—that's all. What I have come to recognize is that just as "the black problem" turned out to be a problem of white racism, just as "the woman problem" turned out to be a problem of male sexism, so "the homosexual problem" is really the homophobia of many heterosexuals. I know gays have hang-ups; so do straights, and I leave these hang-ups to the psychologists. I am appalled at the promiscuity of some gays, but no more appalled than are many other gays. Promiscuity is cruel and degrading in any sexual orientation, but straights bear a special responsibility for the promiscuity of gays. Just as blacks used to be labeled shiftless by whites who made sure there would be no reward for their diligence, so straights call gays promiscuous while denying support for overtly gay stable relationships—the spouse in the parsonage.

So enough of these fixed certainties. If what we think is right and wrong divides still further the human family, there must be something wrong with what we think is right. Enough of this cruelty and hatred, this punitive legislation toward gay people on the part of straight Christians. Claiming to be full of principles, these Christians are proving to be full of prejudice. Peter widened his horizons; let's not narrow ours. It has been said that a mind once stretched by a new idea can never return to its former shape. Let's listen, learn, let's read and pray— none of this is easy—until with Peter's conviction we can make a similar confession: "Truly I perceive that God shows no partiality, but in every sexual orientation any one who fears him and does what is right is acceptable to him."

What Saint Augustine called the duty of the preacher is the obligation of all: "to teach what is right and to re- fute what is wrong, and in the performance of this task to conciliate the hostile [and] to rouse the careless."

Suggested Reading

John Boswell, *Christianity, Social Tolerance, and Homosexuality: Gay People in Western Europe from the Beginning of the Christian Era to the Fourteenth Century* (Chicago: University of Chicago Press, 1980).

Christianity and Crisis, A Special Issue on Homosexuality, May 30 & June 13, 1977.

John McNeill, *The Church and the Homosexual* (Sheed, Andrews & McMeel, 1976).

Letha Scanzoni and Virginia Ramey Mollenkott, *Is the Homosexual My Neighbor? Another Christian View* (San Francisco: Harper & Row, 1978).

6
Abortion

HERE IS good advice: Think thoughts that are as clear as possible, but no clearer; say things as simply as possible, but no simpler. And remember that the answer to the question "What is the opposite of a profound truth?" is "Another profound truth."

Abortion is not only a complex, controversial, and pressing problem, to my way of thinking it is an unyielding dilemma, or at least a dilemma that yields but little, and only to those who accord it the respect due an unyielding dilemma.

Consider, for instance, some of the phrases commonly heard in the abortion debate. Take, for example, "sanctity of life." This phrase can be invoked in favor of fetal rights as well as in favor of the human species' right to survival, threatened as it seems to be by overpopulation. Or take the phrase, "God forbids the taking of innocent life." Patently true and another reason for abolishing warfare in the nuclear age, but that still leaves us human beings to define "innocent" and "life." Or, "We cannot play God." Agreed again. But *God* does not play God, as that phrase is generally understood. God does not intervene directly in our affairs as the primary causative agent of our births and deaths. God does not marry us and take us to bed, any more than God goes around firing every murderer's pistol, sitting behind every steering wheel, smoking every cigarette. Of course we cannot play God, but neither can we pretend we are without responsibility, mere passive victims of whatever befalls us. After all, we are "a royal priesthood, a holy nation, God's own people."

I have said that God wants us to affirm and protect life, more and more of it. God must have been pleased with the social consciousness that finally grew sufficiently sensitive to abolish slavery. God must be pleased today with our long-overdue recognition of the rights of women, the rights of prisoners, soldiers, poor people, the handicapped, children, even whales. Why should we not talk of the rights of the unborn? I think it is fine that we do. That being said, I still see no final, lasting, satisfactory-to-all-sides solution until medical technology becomes so advanced and society so enlightened that abortion is no longer necessary.

Is there any ground for moral consensus? And if not, are there grounds at least for legal consensus? Morally we can agree, I think, that the right to life of a human being is fundamental, and that innocent life should not be taken. If so, then the crucial question is, "At what point, if at any stage, can unborn life be called human?"

The Roman Catholic Church certainly has clear

thoughts on this matter. The Catholic Hospital Association of the United States and Canada has specified: "Every unborn child must be regarded as a human person, with all the rights of a human person, from the moment of conception." That statement commends itself not only for its clarity, but also for its desire to affirm and protect more and more of life, and for its honesty in making the assertion a moral rather than a medical judgment. Medicine cannot tell us when unborn life can be called human. Medical science can tell us when a heart starts beating, just as it can tell us when a heart has stopped beating. But science cannot say when it is morally right to cease all artificial supports of a dying person, because science is not in a position to declare, "This is no longer a human person." That is a moral, not a medical, judgment. The business of science is only to make clear the facts of natural life, not the values of human life.

But is that clear assertion of the Catholic Hospital Association just a little clearer than clarity warrants? There was a time, centuries ago, when the Church was less clear on this matter, a time when theologians tried to distinguish between a fetus that was "formed"—ensouled—and one that was as yet "unformed"—without soul. Writing in the twelfth century, Gratian declared, "He is not a murderer who brings about abortion before the soul is in the body."

That sounds fairly biblical, does it not? "Then the Lord God formed man of dust from the ground, and breathed into his nostrils the breath of life; and man became a living being." The purely physical aspects of life are metaphorically portrayed as dust. But a living soul is more than dust; a living soul is nature—plus! A living soul speaks, reasons, judges between right and wrong. Certainly a fertilized egg in a woman's uterus is human in origin and human in destiny, but is that enough to warrant calling a fertilized egg a human being with a full complement of moral and legal rights? Does the older and less clear developmental view of life not make at least as much sense as the contemporary one that erases all distinctions between potential life and actual life? In fact, do not Roman Catholics, along with all the rest of us, act as if there *were* a difference between potential and actual life? When a fetus aborts spontaneously, we grieve for the parents, hardly at all for the life no one has seen. We do not have funerals for unborn children. And I have never heard anyone urge the same punishment for a mother who aborts a fetus as for one who murders a grown son or daughter.

Troubling too in the contemporary Catholic view of abortion is the divorce of motive and action. I always have trouble with a moral methodology that has so worked out its principles in advance that the specifics in any given case are irrelevant. Suppose a mother in the slums of New York or Caracas, with more children than resources to keep them alive and well, decides on an abortion for the sake of the children she already has. Can her motive have "the moral malice [of murder]"? If every doctor who in good conscience performs an abortion is a murderer, then so is every conscientious soldier. Obviously such labeling is unfair, simplistic. Obviously you can never totally divorce actions and motives. It is not that the end justifies the means, but that ends give meaning to means.

And finally, there is simply insufficient evidence to bear out the claim so frequently made that abortion is dangerous because it threatens the meaning and value of life generally. Japan has the most permissive abortion system in the world, but is life less sacred there than, say, in Argentina or Chile?

Turning now from the moral to the legal aspect of abortion, I think we have to say, first of all, that the legal position generally taken by Roman Catholic bishops is consistent with their moral position. At their best the bishops are not trying to infringe on our religious liberties by imposing Catholic beliefs on non-Catholics. Their opposition to the legalization of abortion is based on their belief that "any law that imperils the right to life of innocent human persons is a social evil." If abortion is murder, then it is a crime; it is that simple. Therefore it makes little sense for Jews, humanists, and Protestants to say to Catholics, "Call abortion a sin, but not a crime." How would you like it if someone said to you, "Call genocide a sin, but not a crime; call a preemptive strike on Russia a sin, but not a crime"?

But again, it is not that simple, and the best of the bishops know it. We are at the heart of the dilemma, but here the dilemma does yield just a bit. In Roman Catholic jurisprudence, for a law to be good it must be shown— among other things—to be enforceable, for unenforced laws tend to bring all law into disrepute. Recognizing that there has been little will and probably no way to enforce antiabortion laws, some Catholics, like Father Robert Drinan in Boston, have brought traditional Catholic legal points to bear in order to lessen traditional Catholic opposition to liberalized abortion laws. The moral position of these Catholics remains the same, but they recognize the lesser of two evils. They know that legalized abortion means more legal abortions. But it also means fewer deaths of women from illegal abortions. Father Drinan has even suggested the removal of abortion from the field of legislation, provided there was an understanding that doctors would not be forced to perform operations to which they were conscientiously opposed.

I have tried to suggest that the right to life of a fetus, from the moment of conception on, is too narrow a basis for determining the morality of abortion. Such a view does not sufficiently differentiate between biological and human life, between potential and actual life; it leaves out altogether the question of motive; and it links abortion in an unpersuasive manner to the devaluation of all life.

Another view, frequently voiced by opponents of the Roman Catholic position, is that whether to have an abortion is a medical question to be decided, like all other medical questions, by the patient and her doctor. Like the earlier statement of the Catholic Hospital Association, this position also commends itself for its clarity. But unlike the statement of the doctors, it shows no desire to affirm and protect more and more of life and reduces the moral judgment of the doctors to a mere medical one. Abortion is certainly a medical procedure, but is it a medical question? If science is in no position to decide when in the uterus natural life becomes human, so science is in no position to decide that unborn life is never human. And it is a bad moral judgment, in my view, to make the value of a fetus solely dependent on whether or not the mother wants it. To be sure, a fetus is part of a woman's body, but it is also *not* part of a woman's body. If a man participated in its origin, and its destiny is to live on its own, how can it be considered *merely* a woman's property and its removal no different from the removal of any other tissue of a woman's body?

It has even been said that a woman's right to an abortion is an absolute right. Whether that means a legal or a moral right is not always clear. What is clear is that absolute rights, whether legal or moral—rights taken out of the framework of all other rights—are what get us into trouble. What is the opposite of a profound truth? Another profound truth. What is the opposite of a human right? Another human right. These are genuine dilemmas, and as I said earlier, the worst thing we can do with a dilemma is to resolve it prematurely because we lack the courage to live with uncertainty. Once again, as with the issue of homosexuality, we have to listen, think and read, pray hard, and reason together—all of us. I am looking forward to the day when abortion is unnecessary. In the meantime I agree with Margaret Mead's characterization of abortion: it is a nasty thing, but our society deserves it.

If we follow Father Drinan's line of reasoning, we may yet reach grounds for legal consensus. Like it or not, we have all of us to recognize that abortions have been a common human practice for a long time; surveying three hundred and fifty societies, George Devereux could find only one in which induced abortion did not occur. Abortions are also very numerous, most being performed on married women. This makes the enforcement of antiabortion laws at least as difficult as the enforcement of Prohibition laws. We also have to remember that antiabortion laws create quack practitioners; they crucify legitimate physicians who must make agonizing decisions between abiding by the law and doing what they consider humane; they create extortionists who "shake down" both legitimate and illegitimate practitioners; they corrupt law enforcement officers; and—what is most important—they bring untold suffering to innumerable women, mostly poor women. As far as I can see, those who crusade for antiabortion laws have not the ghost of a chance of lessening any of the above evils (to which I assume they are as opposed as I am), and for that reason I will not join them.

As to who makes the decision: it seems to me that as long as it is women who become pregnant, and women whom society defines as the primary childbearers, the control over the terms and means of pregnancy and childbirth should belong to women and, in the last analysis, to them alone.

But if the legal side of the matter appears relatively clear, the moral one—under what circumstances to have an abortion—remains complicated. At what point, if at any, can unborn life be called human? I simply cannot answer that. And if I remain as religious as I have been thus far, I may never be able to do so. There are mysteries known only to God; and even "God's own people" should not play God.

Suggested Reading

Daniel Callahan, *Abortion: Law, Choice, and Morality* (New York: Macmillan, 1970).

R. F. R. Gardner, *Abortion—The Personal Dilemma: A Christian Gynecologist Examines the Medical, Social, and Spiritual Issues* (Greenwood, S.C.: Attic Press, 1975).

Lawrence Lader, *Abortion II: Making the Revolution* (Boston: Beacon Press, 1973).

Betty Sarvis and Hyman Rodman, *The Abortion Controversy* (New York & London: Columbia University Press, 1973).

7

The Promised Time

EARLIER, I quoted a novelist's suggestion that "greed for personal salvation . . . might be the most obnoxious greed there is." Salvation, of course, is personal, but it is not private. Nor is it exclusive, at someone else's expense. No, salvation is for everyone—including me. "Not til the sun excludes you do I exclude you": Whitman's words to outcasts the Lord could address to each and every one of us. Moreover, salvation is a package deal that cannot be untied or negotiated; it includes politics, economics, the past, the present, and particularly the future.

I want now to think large thoughts, and to get us started, let us recall the story in the thirteenth and fourteenth chapters of the Book of Numbers. Here we read that after a long and tearstained trek, the Children of Israel finally reach the borders of the Promised Land. Spies are sent out, and when they return they give a majority report and a minority report. The minority report, submitted by Joshua and Caleb, is prophetic; it says, in effect, "We can go ahead, we can do God's will if only we do not lose hope," which we can characterize as "a passion for the possible." The majority report, as one might expect, is pragmatic. The prudence it counsels only thinly veils the cowardice of those submitting it. It speaks of "giants" in the land—the sons of Anak (literally, "the long-necked one"): "And we seemed to ourselves like grasshoppers and so we seemed to them."

Predictably, the Children of Israel accept the majority report. We read, "All the congregation raised a loud cry; and the people wept that night. And all the people of Israel murmured against Moses and Aaron; the whole congregation said to them, 'Would that we had died in the land of Egypt!...' And they said to one another, 'Let us choose a captain, and go back to Egypt.'" When Aaron and Moses remonstrate, and Caleb and Joshua get up once again and say, "The Lord is with us," all the congregation can think to do is stone them.

I have two reasons for recalling this story. The first is the line, "We seemed to ourselves like grasshoppers." It reflects the constant problem we have been talking about: fear. The story shows that while love seeks truth, fear seeks safety. And fear distorts the truth not by exaggerating the ills of the world (which would be difficult), but by underestimating our ability to deal with them: "We seemed to ourselves like grasshoppers." What we see here is the protective strategy of deliberate failure: you can't lose any money if you don't place any bets; you can't fall out of bed if you sleep on the floor. Further, if you think other people—those giants—are responsible for making you a failure, then you do not have to feel bad about being one. And finally, if you think those trying to wean you from your sense of failure—the Calebs and Joshuas of the world—are only trying to push you around, you can, with good conscience, stone them.

The second reason for recalling the story is that while I do not think there is a Promised Land for anybody any more, I believe there is a Promised Time for everybody. After a far longer and even more arduous trek, the three billion of us and more who inhabit this planet are in fact on the very borders of that time promised in Scripture— "it shall come to pass in the latter days"—when, if we do not lose our passion for the possible, we might indeed create a world without famine; a world, in effect, without borders; a world, at last, at one and at peace.

But instead of pressing forward, God's children once again are holding back. Instead of "seizing the time" we are losing our grip. It is understandable. We have been through tough, disillusioning times. (Who was it who said, "I used to be an incurable optimist, but now I'm cured"?) And I understand why we are fearful: Ahead *are* giants. But what are giant obstacles if not brilliant opportunities brilliantly disguised as giant obstacles? Even in the deep darkness of winter, don't Christians know in their hearts an invincible summer?

My favorite definition of patriotism is the one offered by an ancient Roman, Tacitus, who said that patriotism is entering into praiseworthy competition with our ancestors. I think we should enter into praiseworthy competition with Moses and Joshua and with Washington and Jefferson. They declared their independence, the first two from Egypt, the second two from England. Let us declare, in contrast, our *inter*dependence with all people. Let us dare to see pragmatically that the survival unit in our time is no longer an individual nation or an individual anything. The survival unit in our time is the whole human race.

It used to be that we worried about one part of the globe not being able to protect itself from another part. In the nuclear age it is the whole that cannot protect itself from the parts. It used to be that a nation could solve its own problems; today there are no major problems that are not both interrelated and international. We can no longer say that the individual nation-state is the principal focus for thought and action. Responsible national citizenship has to give way to international citizenship. And that pragmatic view is, of course, the same as the ancient prophetic view, according to which all of us belong one to another, all three billion of us. That is the way God made us. Christ died to keep us that way. Our sin is only that we are always trying to put asunder what God himself has joined together. "Am I my brother's keeper?" No, I am my brother's brother, or sister. Human unity is not something we are called on to create, only to recognize. What we have to recognize—and quickly make manifest—is that territorial discrimination is as evil as racial discrimination. God cares for all as if all were but one; or as Saint Paul said, "There is neither Jew nor Greek . . . for you are all one in Christ Jesus."

But God also cares for each as if there were no one else to care for. Do you remember how Jesus asks, "Are not five sparrows sold for two pennies?" He is referring to the practice of sacrifice, and to the poor who could not afford bullocks. They would buy two sparrows for a penny, and if they bought two pennies worth—four sparrows—a fifth was thrown in free. God cares for that fifth sparrow! And Jesus goes on to say, "You are of more value than many sparrows."

"Not til the sun excludes you do I exclude you." It is not enough then to talk merely of interdependence. Many people have been doing that for some time: the Trilateral Commission, for example, and presidents of multinational corporations who are quick to say that national boundaries are no more interesting to them than is the equator. But the powerful of the world tend naturally to see themselves as the elders of the global village. They tend to see a unity based on the present order that favors their privileged position, rather than a unity based on greater justice for the poor and the powerless. History has shown that the rich and powerful are far more willing to alleviate the results of poverty than to attack its causes, that their primary preoccupation is always with order rather than justice. But history has also shown that concern for disorder over injustice invariably produces more of both. It has been said that those who make peaceful evolution impossible make violent revolution inevitable. It is not enough to envisage a global future. A world at peace demands a *just* and global future, one that reflects the words of the Magnificat: "He has put down the

mighty from their thrones, and exalted those of low degree; he has filled the hungry with good things, and the
rich he has sent empty away."

As much of what I have just said would seem to spell
bad news for many Americans, let me quickly recall an
often forgotten fact: judgment of the rich spells mercy not
only for the poor, but finally for the rich as well. There
are two ways to be rich. One is to have lots of money, the
other to have few needs. Whereas the second option is
rarely weighed in the United States, the Bible promotes it
all the time, suggesting, moreover, that spiritual resources—the only truly renewable resources—do better
when economic ones are not in excess.

Consider this: the United States, with only 5.8 percent
of the world's population, currently consumes about 35
percent of the world's resources. Were we Americans profoundly happy, I suppose it would be argued—by some—
that such is the price the rest of the world must pay for
American happiness. But we are not a profoundly happy
people. Our affluence has not bought morale. In fact, it
has bought a great deal of loneliness and emptiness as
our acquisitiveness has disrupted our sense of community. So if the wealth of rich Americans must be redistribut-
ed at home and abroad in order to eliminate gross in-
equalities—if some degree of austerity is called for—all is
well. We need not view austerity as a necessary evil, only
as a necessary ingredient for that sense of community of
which we see all too little among our own people and
among the nations.

And how do we proceed from here? I am not sure. A
Law of the Sea, a small standing army at the service of

the UN, an international income tax based on energy consumption or military budgets—all these seem possible first steps. I do know Christians should never lose their passion for the possible, and Christians should be urging the world to continue its exodus from the old time to the new. The road is hard but the future is bright. The Promised Time is there ahead; already we can dimly view its contours. The spies are back, the prophetic ones among them proclaiming that the Promised Time will be a vast improvement over the good old days. So enough of this "back to Egypt" talk. Enough of this nonsense about seeming to ourselves like grasshoppers. We too can become giants, Anaks—simply by sticking out our necks. We have created a world for some of us. It is time now to make one for all of us.

Suggested Reading

Robert McAfee Brown, *Making Peace in the Global Village* (Philadelphia: Westminster Press, 1981).

8

The Arms Race

BUT THERE will be no world for any of us unless we stop the mad momentum of the arms race. For years both the United States and the Soviet Union have possessed nuclear arsenals capable of annihilating humanity. That is what I meant by saying "the whole cannot protect itself from the parts." Just think—the whole world now lives on the target! Yet both sides—the Soviet Union and the United States—continue to produce nuclear warheads at the rate of about three a day. It makes common sense blush. We are like alcoholics who know that liquor is killing them, but who can always find a good reason to take another drink.

Every day there are fewer military solutions. It is ridiculous to talk of the "defense" budget or the "defense" department when there is no defense in the nuclear age. Every attempt to enhance our security by accelerating the arms race has inexorably diminished that security until the Soviet Union and the United States are both weak to the point of helplessness before the threat of a nuclear holocaust. To avoid that holocaust we have to declare that nuclear war simply is not war; it is suicide, and hence a matter not for statesmen and generals to plan but for citizens to prevent. As for those who talk of limited nuclear war, they are like someone walking into an ammunition dump, lighting a match, and saying, "Don't worry; I'm just going to blow up a few mortar rounds."

Why is it so hard to see that either we put an end to war or war will put an end to us? In the fourth chapter of Luke, the devil takes Jesus up to a high place, and after showing him "all the kingdoms of the world in a moment of time" says to him, "To you I will give all this authority and their glory; for it has been delivered to me." (An interesting view of worldly power!) Then the devil makes his proposal: "If you, then, will worship me, it shall all be yours." And Jesus, using Scripture as a sword to parry the thrusts of the devil, answers, "You shall worship the Lord your God, and him only shall you serve."

Once, in preparing for a sermon on this passage, I took a piece of paper and wrote on one side, "Service to the Lord," and on the other, "Service to the devil." Then I asked myself, "What is the bottom line if you are serious about serving the Lord on the one hand, and the devil on the other?" On the Lord's side of the paper, the matter resolved itself quickly: if we fail in love, we fail in all things else.

On the devil's side the question seemed more complicated. But rereading the temptation story, it occurred to me that the one thing you cannot be without if you are serious about serving the devil is power. The temptation is to seek status through power.

Suddenly it hit me. The devil has taken over two hundred million of us Americans up to a high place, has shown us "all the kingdoms of the world in a moment of time," and is whispering in our ears: "Now let's see, Americans. You have enough weapons to kill everyone in the world many times over, and you're still turning out three nuclear warheads a day—terrific!—you can always bounce the rubble. And it only takes warheads thirty minutes to go door to door, so that soon you and the Soviets will have to adopt what your Pentagon calls a 'launch-upon-warning' strategy, which gives over the decision-making power to the impersonal province of those imperfect computers that make all those mistakes—it sounds wonderful! And you and the Soviets are going for a first-strike capability. Marvelous! That should make everyone as nervous as a cat in a room full of rocking chairs. Just think, Americans: one of these days you and the Soviets might destroy all the kingdoms of the world in a moment of time—*by accident.*"

Let me describe what would happen to the island of Manhattan were New Yorkers to be hit by a mere twenty-megaton nuclear bomb. First of all there would be an incredible flash of heat and light. In less than a second, the temperature would rise to 150 million degrees Fahrenheit—four times the temperature at the center of the sun. A roar would immediately follow, but in the center of the city no one would hear it. There would be nothing left but heat and dust.

The explosion would bore a crater in solid rock— Manhattan is solid granite—deep enough to contain a twenty-story building. The crater would be a mile and a half wide. At ground zero, in less than one second, every-thing—skyscrapers, roads, bridges, some million people— would instantly evaporate. Within three seconds the fire-ball would reach a height and breadth of about four miles, and its flash would be bright enough to blind the crew of an incoming airliner as far as a hundred miles away. After sixty seconds the familiar shape of the mush-room cloud would begin to form, expanding for ten or fifteen minutes, reaching a height of about twenty-five miles, and extending some eighty miles across the sky.

To a distance of five miles from ground zero there would be—nothing. To a distance of ten miles, winds up to a thousand miles per hour would hurl flaming cars and trucks into the air like grotesque Molotov cocktails, spewing gasoline, oil, and shrapnel everywhere in their path. Twenty miles away people would suffer first-de-gree burns. A firestorm would soon rage beyond control. Fallout could cover an area of about forty-eight hundred square miles, depending on the wind. Lethal radiation would contaminate the area for as long as two months, then subside to high but not immediately lethal levels for as long as ten months.

Picture similar scenes across the face of the land. Would the living not envy the dead? According to Helen Caldicott and Physicians for Social Responsibility, the answer is yes. The lack of medicine, food, and housing would be a nightmare. Deformities would continue for generations, assuming that the ozone depletion did not make the earth uninhabitable.

I have two great fears. I am afraid that nuclear war is a possibility simply too grisly to be taken seriously. This would account for the continued apathy and fatalism of the majority of civilians, who leave the game to the military—so many of whom live cocooned from the real world. And I am afraid that the devil is seducing us to seek status through power. The one thing we Americans are not about to give up is power. "We're Number One!"—is that not the cry going up from every redblooded American heart?

In March 1979, *Business Week* devoted an entire issue to the decline of U.S. power. On the cover was the face of one of my favorite women in all the world, the Statue of Liberty, and down her right cheek was coursing a single great tear. When I was a kid, I was taught that this was a statue to American liberty, not to American power. And if our lady of the harbor is weeping, it may be because of the irrational love of loveless power that has gripped the hearts and minds of so many of us Americans.

To prove that the logic of our defense policies can be outmoded as swiftly as they are promulgated, Professor Lloyd Etheredge of MIT recently wrote that we like to picture ourselves over here, the Soviets over there. With our respective deterrences we think we can keep each other's warheads where they belong—at home. But soon nuclear bombs will be portable. Only slightly larger than baseballs, they will be able to be hidden in diplomatic pouches, in the tutus of the Bolshoi Ballet. Neither side will know when and where they will be in place—in the United States and in the Soviet Union. Nor, if they go off, will either side know who set them off. So, according to Professor Etheredge, sophisticated discussions about early radar warnings, long range delivery missiles, satellite laser gun technology, new penetration aids, are all quite pointless.

I think it is pointless for any nation to try to be Number One in the nuclear age. "Superiority" is a concept without substance. So instead of to the devil, we should be listening to Einstein, who years ago warned: "The release of the power of the atom has changed everything, except our way of thinking. Thus we drift towards a catastrophe of unparalleled magnitude." Instead of the devil we should be heeding the psalmist: "The war horse is a vain hope for victory, and by its great might it cannot save." Instead of escalating the arms race, we should be doing everything we possibly can to slow, stop, and reverse it. This is the meat-and-potatoes issue of our day, and it is on the plate of every Christian.

Suggested Reading

Dale Aukerman, *The Darkening Valley* (New York: Seabury Press, 1981).

Richard Barnet, *Real Security: Restoring American Power in a Dangerous Decade* (New York: Simon & Schuster, 1981).

Mary Kaldor, *The Baroque Arsenal* (New York: Hill & Wang, 1981).

Sidney Lens, *The Day Before Doomsday: An Anatomy of the Nuclear Arms Race* (Boston: Beacon Press, 1978).

E. P. Thompson and Dan Smith, eds., *Protest and Survive* (New York & London: Monthly Review Press, 1981).

Note: For further information on reversing the arms race, write to: Riverside Church Disarmament Program, 490 Riverside Drive, New York, N.Y. 10027.

9

The

Soviets

"BUT WHAT about the Russians, Reverend? Can you trust them?" (And of course on the other side they have the same question: "All well and good, Comrade, but how can you trust those Americans?")

Wars always begin in the mind. You have first to *think* others to death. You cannot kill a brother. You cannot kill a sister, a friend, a fellow human being. But you can kill a Marxist, a capitalist, an imperialist, a leftist guerrilla.

More accurately, wars begin in the heart when fear—once again—displaces love. To induce fear is the worst possible way to avoid conflict: "Fear begets suspicion and distrust and evil imaginings of all sorts til each government feels that it would be criminal and the betrayal of its country not to take every precaution, while every government regards the precaution of every other government as evidence of hostile intent." Those words, spoken before World War I by British Foreign Minister Sir Edward Grey, describe the double standard of today. They do something, it is evil; we do the same thing, it is necessary for national security. Or how about this: our satellite interceptors have the acronym SAINTS; theirs we call "killer satellites."

For years the Soviet Union and the United States have lived in mutual fear. For years deterrence has been the watchword. But on both sides a tremendous error has been made in thinking deterrence a stationary state. As the British historian E. P. Thompson has pointed out, deterrence is not a stationary state; it is a degenerative state. The repressed violence backs up into each nation's politics, economics, ideology, and culture. Fear increases selfish loves. Fear refines ever more hideous weapons. Fear enlarges the government's control over its population and its client states. As I write this, the Soviets are menacing the Poles, and the United States is threatening every guerrilla (others call them "freedom fighters") in Central America. Without doubt, the renewed Cold War of the 1980s is reinforcing the ugliest features in both societies. And we must remember a psychological factor: expectation without action becomes boring; so psychologically we are always pushed to fulfill our expectations. Is this why nuclear war, once unthinkable, is again thinkable— even winnable, we are told? What Hiroshima and Nagasaki had begun to delegitimize, we are now relegitimizing. We are putting a foundation back under a condemned building.

"You have heard that it was said, 'You shall love your

neighbor and hate your enemy.' But I say to you, 'Love your enemies.' " As if in anticipation of Soviet-American relations, and as a commentary on Christ's command, Yeats once wrote:

> We had fed the heart on fantasies,
> The heart's grown brutal from the fare;
> More substance in our enmities
> Than in our love. . . .

It may be too much to ask of a whole nation that it love its enemy. Nevertheless, no one—no Christian at least—can justify changing the divine commandment to love your enemy into an imperative to hate all communists. Nor is there any justification for bearing false witness against your neighbors just because they are your enemies. Governments are like individuals: they oversimplify things that make them angry. Still, there is no excusing Ronald Reagan's statement: "Let us not delude ourselves, the Soviet Union underlies all the unrest that is going on. If they weren't engaged in this game of dominoes, there wouldn't be any hot spots in the world."

When I first read those words, I tried to imagine what it would be like as an American to be told, "If you want to understand the present discontent of blacks in the United States, you do not have to examine its roots in slavery or to analyze what survived slavery, personal and institutional racism. No, it is enough to look for outside agitators who came into our country to make trouble and where possible to seduce naive blacks, like Paul Robeson, into becoming communists." Even the most bigoted segregationist would balk at that explanation. Yet regarding the Third World, that is the line we are asked to swallow: "Let us not delude ourselves, the Soviet Union underlies all the unrest that is going on."

In Scripture we read that God visits "the iniquity of the fathers upon the children unto the third and fourth generation." That is not a statement of fairness, but a statement of fact—declaring that our actions have consequences, not only laterally across the face of one generation, but also vertically down the march of generations. That means, concerning violence in our ghettos, that you can only understand it by understanding first the original injustice that put people in the ghettos and now keeps them there (which is not to say that criminals are always poor, or that there are not poor people living blameless lives amid the misery of ghettos). With respect to the Third World it means that if you want to understand Castro, you must go back and look at Batista. If you want to know what happened in the Dominican Republic, check out Trujillo. If you want to know what happened in Vietnam, remember the French, Emperor Bao Dai, and Diem. If you want to know what happened in Nicaragua, look at Somoza. And if you want to know what is going on today in El Salvador, mention Cuban guns if you like, say the Soviet Union is imperialistic (it most definitely is), but don't say "the Soviet Union underlies all the unrest." As early as 1932 (all but ignored by our press and forgotten today by the American public) Salvadoran peasants, artisans, and workers, armed only with machetes and stones, rose up against their misery. Within a month thirty thousand of them had been slaughtered. Since then conditions have improved but little. So let us indeed not delude ourselves: you cannot have a revolt without revolting conditions. Communism has never come to a nation that took care of its poor, its aged, its youth, its sick, and its handicapped.

Most of all, regarding our enemies we have this to consider: if we are not one with them in love, at least we are one with them in sin—which is no mean bond, because it precludes the possibility of separation through judgment. That is the meaning of "Judge not, that ye be not judged." Fight evil, yes, but never as if evil were something that arose totally outside of yourself. Americans, properly incensed not only at the Soviet treatment of dissidents, which is outrageous, but also at the Soviet invasion of Afghanistan, and before that, of Czechoslovakia and Hungary, should remember that we have made no few mistakes ourselves when it comes to intervening unilaterally in the internal affairs of other nations. And we threaten to make more. "If we value our freedom, we must be able to defend ourselves in wars of any size and shape and in any region where we have vital interests," Casper Weinberger has said. In recent years both the Soviet Union and the United States have passed from isolationism into interventionism—without passing through internationalism. Neither has any right to regard the mote in the other's eye with no concern for the beam in its own. The danger in so doing is transparent: if we consider ourselves sinless, and the Soviets the devil (with whom you should never strike a bargain), then we will never seriously negotiate; and if we insist that the only thing they understand is force, then we will *behave* as if the only thing *we* understand is force—which is pretty much what we are doing now.

Safety for the world, not vengeance on a foe, must be our motive. The Soviet Union is not Enemy Number One. Enemy Number One is a nuclear holocaust, and the Soviets are our most serious adversaries—with whom we have to negotiate, and negotiate, and negotiate. As for communism, if it is true that it has never come to a nation that took care of its aged, its youth, its sick, and its handicapped, if it is true that communism is essentially a parasite that feeds on disease in the body politic, then the smart way to fight communism is to fight poverty, illiteracy, unemployment, and illness.

Most Americans regard the Soviet Union as a state at the service of communism. I would contend the contrary, that in the Soviet Union communism is an ideology at the service of the state. I am impressed that the Soviet Union is now the only nation in all the world surrounded by hostile communist countries. Beyond being intensely nationalistic, the Soviet Union is also a typical superpower. In other words, the Soviets are dangerous to the world not because their society is different from ours, but because in foreign policy, at least, we are so similar. Like all great powers, both countries are greedy for influence and glory in their power, and for that reason, make hideous mistakes. The Soviet Union has undoubtedly made more anticommunists than we, and we have made more communists than they. Yet to reduce our respective nuclear arsenals is in the interest of both sides, and I think the Soviets know this better than we. In 1945 theirs was a mired, ravaged country. Over twenty million Russians died in the war, and that memory is very much alive in Russian minds almost forty years later. Leonid Brezhnev's own cardiologist was given a half hour on Soviet television to describe the horrors of nuclear war to a nationwide audience. Would that an American doctor would be invited to do the same on American television.

Moreover, every Soviet citizen I have ever met knows that what the American right wing is saying about their alleged military superiority is arrant nonsense. Parity may be asymmetrical, but when all the warheads are tallied in all the countries that have them, far more of these weapons are anti-Soviet than pro-Soviet. And finally, the Soviets know better than we how devastating to the economy of every nation the arms race is. So the failure we need fear is less the failure to meet a threat, more the failure to meet an opportunity. Why have we not put our best minds to work on arms reduction? Why have we not invited third parties to help us the way we do in resolving domestic disputes? Why have we not taken unilateral initiatives for bilateral disarmament in order to prove that our stated willingness to negotiate is accompanied by a serious desire to disarm?

Arms reduction cannot await the end of Soviet-American rivalry; it is the rivalry that makes arms reduction necessary. To those who say, "Now is not the time to talk," the answer is, "We haven't a day to lose." To those who think that in the nuclear age to look and act tough is true grit, the answer is, "That's foolish grit, a determined blindness of heart."

Can we trust the Russians? Can they trust us? Finally,

have we any choice? Fear can arm us, but fear can never disarm us. Only trust can do that. The safety of the world hangs on the hope that both nations will be rational enough to act in their own self-interest.

There is a nice story told of Heinrich Heine, the German (or Jewish) poet, who was standing with a friend before the cathedral of Amiens in France. "Tell me, Heinrich," said his friend, "why can't people build piles like this any more?"

"My dear friend," replied Heine, "in those days people had convictions. We moderns have opinions. And it takes more than an opinion to build a Gothic cathedral."

There is no question that almost all Russians and Americans want peace. But peace in our minds is an opinion, not a conviction. We—most of us—are hearers of the Word, not doers; we wish for peace, but we do not *will* it. We want peace in our shopping baskets, along with military superiority and a few other things that make peace impossible. We are like Kaiser Wilhelm, who is supposed to have remarked, "We do not want war, we want only victory."

Said Cyrus Vance in 1980 at Harvard: "History may conclude that ours was a failure not of opportunity but of seeing opportunity; a failure not of resources but of wisdom to use them; a failure not of intellect but of understanding and of *will*" (emphasis added).

If our wills are not paralyzed, but freed at last by the eternal dispenser of freedom, the eternal dispenser of life, we *will* from now on regard every human being as a child of God. In each we will see a sister or a brother— and a Russian, American, Marxist, or capitalist at a later, more convenient hour. And we *will* continue to do so because he who came to show us the way will also see us through.

Suggested Reading

Richard Barnet, *The Giants: Russia and the United States* (New York: Simon & Schuster, 1978).

George F. Kennan, "A Proposal for International Disarmament," address delivered upon accepting the Albert Einstein Peace Prize, May 19, 1981, Washington, D.C.

10

Beating
Burn-Out

AN OLD man in India sat down in the shade of an ancient banyan tree whose roots disappeared far away in a swamp. Presently he discerned a commotion where the roots entered the water. Concentrating his attention, he saw that a scorpion had become helplessly entangled in the roots. Pulling himself to his feet, he made his way carefully along the tops of the roots to the place where the scorpion was trapped. He reached down to extricate it. But each time he touched the scorpion, it lashed his hand with its tail, stinging him painfully. Finally his hand was so swollen he could no longer close his fingers, so he withdrew to the shade of the tree to wait for the swelling to go down. As he arrived at the trunk, he saw a young man standing above him on the road laughing at him. "You're a fool," said the young man, "wasting your time trying to help a scorpion that can only do you harm." The old man replied, "Simply because it is in the nature of the scorpion to sting, should I change my nature, which is to save?"

I told that story in a sermon one Sunday, and moved myself nearly to tears. Immediately after the service two of our ever-alert choir members came up to register their reactions. Said a soprano of invincible practicality, "Why didn't the old man use a stick?" (I'd like to hear her sing an aria dedicated to a stung stick.) Said a contralto with a considerable reputation for social activism, "What happens when your hand gets so infected it falls off? We need a sermon on burn-out."

It used to be that when people said "I feel burned out," they were describing their personal exhaustion and frustration with their careers or marriages. But today "burn-out" also describes a condition common to those who thought that on such issues as the environment, peace, poverty, and human rights they had built something solid on hard rock only to find out that the rock was sand. Burn-out is a common condition for those who think that points once proved should stay proved, that progress is an arrow, not a pendulum. It is burn-out when you feel like Rocinante, a tired hack of a horse ridden by a Quixotic idea. It is burn-out when you feel like a fly in the evening of its only day of life—tired from the struggle. It is burn-out when all you want to do is quit.

As a remedy for burn-out, let me offer three images of the Church, which to me represent the Church at its best. The first is biblical, that of a pilgrim people who have decided never to arrive. It is an exhausting thought, yet one true to our lives, where change is as insistent as sin and taxes. And it is true to our faith. Ours is a God, after all, who declares, "Behold, I make all things new." Ours is a God of history—a history characterized by an Exodus; one that proclaims a New Testament, that hails a new heaven and a new earth; one that describes a New Jerusalem, anticipates a new song and new wine, and promises that we shall become new beings. For God is ahead of us as much as above us and within us. God gives us the "growth choice" as opposed to the "fear choice," to use Maslow's terms; God gives us a present with a future, and a future right up to the very end of life, for "though our outer nature is wasting away, our inner nature is being renewed every day." Even death is only a horizon, and a horizon is nothing save the limit of our sight: "Weep not, I shall not die. And as I leave the land of the dying I trust to see the blessings of the Lord in the land of the living."

One problem with the Moral Majority is that it offers everyone a present that has only a past. Like the ancient children of Israel, the Moral Majority seeks to elect captains to lead us back to the spiritual slavery of Egypt. Theirs is the fear choice, not the growth choice. They want to go back to the time when the United States owned the Panama Canal; back to the time when we were the undisputed military power of the world; back to the time when women were in the kitchen and gays were in the closet. Back, back, back! They are so "backward" they are all flustered about teaching children the origin of the species, instead of worrying about whether any of our children have a future other than as nuclear ash.

In contrast, let us look forward with the courage of our conviction that the Church at its best is always in an exodus. We are a pilgrim people, a people who have decided never to arrive, a people who live by hope, energized not by what we already possess but by that which is promised: "Behold, I create new heavens and a new earth."

Sure, it's tiring; and it's tough. Imagination comes harder than memory, and faithfulness is more demanding than success. But so what if we fail? Remember, we are not required to finish the task—any more than we are allowed to put it aside.

Let us move on to a second biblical image, that of a prophetic minority. The Bible knows nothing of a moral majority. It assumes that the individual conscience, as opposed to the mass mind, best reflects the universal conscience of humankind. And the Bible insists that a prophetic minority always has more to say to a nation than any majority, silent, moral, or any other. As a matter of fact, majorities in the Bible generally end up stoning the prophets, which suggests that democracies are based less on the proven goodness of the people than on the proven evil of dictators.

What must a prophetic minority do? Essentially as did Jeremiah and all the prophets—speak truth to power. As I said earlier, nations, like individuals, oversimplify the things that make them angry. Their ideological commitments distort their perceptions and deaden their moral sensibilities. We have seen this for years in the Soviet government. (Of the leader of Polish Solidarity, *Pravda* does not ask, "Who is Lech Walesa?" but rather, "Whom does Lech Walesa consciously or unconsciously serve?" Answer: "U.S. imperialists.") But communism is far from the only blinding ideology in the world, and when it comes to sacred symbols, unexamined slogans, and presuppositions, the more powerful ideology may be the anticommunism reflected in Latin American dictatorships, in past and present regimes in Washington, and, sad to say, in many religious circles. In my own lifetime I have seen blind anticommunism produce many legends and lies that led to many unnecessary deaths. The Gulf of Tonkin resolution that brought us into Vietnam in a big way was based on a legend. What took us into the Dominican Republic in 1965 was a lie. Both times we oversimplified things that made us angry. Both times we saw red—in each sense of the word. So in the name of God, and for the sake of God's children who are going to be needlessly slaughtered, a prophetic minority must always be ready to speak out clearly and pay up personally. At the same time, we must pray for grace to contend against wrong without becoming wrongly contentious, grace to fight pretensions of national righteousness without personal self-righteousness. If you love good you have to hate evil; otherwise you are sentimental. But if you hate evil more than you love good, you simply become a damn good hater, and of such people the world has enough.

I said I had three images of the Church. The last is nonbiblical, and it is really a bit cute, but here it is. There is an ad for a bubble bath for children that suggests that it can be almost as much fun to get clean as it is to get dirty. That strikes me as a good ad for a church, for while it recognizes a certain fun in wrongdoing, it also acknowledges that it is a joy to scrub one's mind and soul—and the world—of dirt. It really is a joy—a bubbly joy—to be with irrepressible people who are so precisely because they know and love the Lord. It is a joy to be loved. It is a joy to love others. Of course it is hard to keep going, if only because unwarranted despair is as hard to avoid as wishful thinking. But what do you want—lifetime membership in the Bystanders Association?

"Que Diós no nos dé paz, y sí, gloria." May God deny us peace, but give us glory. I am glad Unamuno put it in the plural, recognizing perhaps that tyrannies are most secure when their victims feel most alone. There is no need to be victimized alone. Christians are like spokes in a wheel: the closer they come to the center, the closer they are to each other. And Unamuno is right: believers are ordained to unrest. In *Waiting for Godot*, Vladimir asks Pozo: "Where are you going?" All unwittingly, Pozo gives the Christian answer: "ON."

A Prayer for Peace

O God, who hast created a world beautiful beyond any singing of it, gratefully we acknowledge that of thy fullness have we received, grace upon grace. Grant now that we may be responsible in the measure that we have received.

Keep us eager to pursue truth beyond the outermost limits of human thought, scornful of the cowardice that dares not face new truth, the laziness content with half-truth, and the arrogance that thinks it knows all truth.

Strengthen our resolve to see fulfilled, the world around and in our time, all hopes for justice so long deferred, and keep us on the stony, long, and lonely road that leads to peace. May we think for peace, struggle for peace, suffer for peace. Fill our hearts with courage that we not give in to bitterness and self-pity, but learn rather to count pain and disappointment, humiliation and setback, as but straws on the tide of life.

So may we run and not grow weary, walk and not faint, until that day when by thy grace faith and hope will be outdistanced by sight and possession, and love will be all in all in this wonderful, terrible, beautiful world.

Amen.

Notes

Introduction

Page	Line	
1	12	Nathaniel Hawthorne, *The House of the Seven Gables*.
3	4	Luke 1:46–55.
3	17	1 Corinthians 12:21, RSV.
4	2	Jim Wallis, *The Call to Conversion* (San Francisco: Harper & Row, 1981).
4	6	1 Corinthians 12:12, RSV.
4	14	*Didache.*
5	9	Martin Marty, *Context*, July 15, 1980.
5	24	John 3:1–30.
7	1	1 John 4:18, RSV.
7	10	Rollo May, *The Courage to Create* (New York: W. W. Norton, 1975).
7	14	Rainer Maria Rilke, *Letters to a Young Poet*, rev. ed. (New York: W. W. Norton, 1963).
8	7	Genesis 3:9, KJV.
8	7	1 Kings 19:9, KJV.
8	12	1 John 4:16, RSV.
8	18	John 15:12, RSV.

Chapter 1. The Courage to Love

9	8	Mark 2:1–12, RSV.
10	25	Proverbs 12:21, RSV.
10	27	Psalm 121:2, KJV.
14	13	Sheldon Kopp, *If You Meet the Buddha on the Road, Kill Him!* (New York: Bantam, 1976).
15	21	1 Corinthians 2:9, KJV.

Chapter 2. The Limits of Life

Page	Line	
18	2	James Thurber, *The Thirteen Clocks* (New York: Simon & Schuster, 1977).
19	23	Sam Keen, *Beginnings Without End* (San Francisco: Harper & Row, 1977).
21	11	Alexander Hamilton (1787). Quoted in "The Rise of Militarism, the Decline of Liberty," *Christianity and Crisis*, October 19, 1981.
21	29	John 19:30, RSV.
22	8	1 Corinthians 3:21–23, KJV.

Chapter 3. Thorns in the Flesh

25	1	2 Corinthians 12:7–10.
26	23	William Blake, *Marriage of Heaven and Hell*, 3.
26	28	Abot de Rabbi Nathan, Chapter 23 (Tannaitic and Amoraic sayings, collected in Gaonic period).
27	31	Matthew 5:5, RSV.
28	17	2 Corinthians 4:7–10, RSV.

Chapter 4. Being Called

31	6	Francine du Plessix Gray, *World Without End* (New York: Simon & Schuster, 1981).
32	8	Matthew 25:40, KJV.
32	19	Psalm 94:3–4, KJV.
34	9	Luke 4:18, RSV.
35	11	Jeremiah 1:6, RSV.
35	27	René Descartes, *Le Discours de la méthode*.
37	11	1 John 3:16, RSV.

Chapter 5. Homosexuality

40	16	Leviticus 11:41–42, RSV.
40	28	Acts 10:34–35, RSV.
41	9	James B. Nelson, "Homosexuality and the Church: Toward a Social Ethics of Love," *Christianity and Crisis*, April 4, 1977.
41	21	Leviticus 18:22, RSV.
43	3	Ezekiel 16:49, RSV.
43	13	Luke 10:10, 12, RSV.

Page Line
44   8   John Money, "Statement on Antidiscrimination Re-
               garding Sexual Orientation," *SIECUS Report* 6 (Septem-
               ber 1977), p. 3.
46   24   Saint Augustine, *On Christian Doctrine.*

Chapter 6. Abortion

50   11   1 Peter 2:9 RSV.
51   2   "Ethical and Religious Directives for Catholic Hospi-
               tals" (St. Louis: The Catholic Hospital Association of
               the United States and Canada, 1965), p. 4.
51   24   *Decretum* (1140). Quoted in Daniel Callahan, *Abortion:
               Law, Choice, and Morality* (New York: Macmillan, 1970),
               p. 411.
51   27   Genesis 2:7, RSV.
52   26   T. J. O'Donnell, "Abortion: II (Moral Aspect)," New
               Catholic Encyclopedia (New York: McGraw-Hill, 1967),
               Vol. I, p. 29.
53   16   "Relaxation of Maryland's Abortion Law Opposed by
               Bishops," statement issued by Cardinal Lawrence She-
               han of Baltimore, Cardinal Patrick O'Boyle of Wash-
               ington, D.C., and Monsignor Paul J. Taggart, Adminis-
               trator of the Diocese of Wilmington, Delaware, *Catholic
               Mind* 66 (March 1968), pp. 1–2.
56   1   George Devereux, "A Typological Study of Abortion in
               350 Primitive, Ancient, and Industrial Societies," in
               *Therapeutic Abortion: Medical, Psychiatric, Anthropological,
               and Religious Considerations,* ed. Harold Rosen (New
               York: Julian Press, 1954).

Chapter 7. The Promised Time

59   6   Walt Whitman, "To a Common Prostitute."
61   14   Jeremiah 49:39, KJV.
62   23   Genesis 4:9, RSV.
62   29   Galatians 3:28, RSV.
63   2   Luke 12:6, RSV.
63   8   Luke 12:7, RSV.
63   30   Luke 1:52, RSV.

Chapter 8. The Arms Race

68   14   Luke 4:1–13, RSV.

Page	Line	
69	25	Richard McSorley, S.J., *Kill? For Peace?* rev. ed. (Washington, D.C.: Center for Peace Studies, 1977); "The Medical Aspects of Nuclear War," pamphlet, Physicians for Social Responsibility (Box 144, Watertown, Mass. 02172).
71	24	Lloyd Etheredge, "The Old Imagery of War Is Outdated," *New York Times,* May 27, 1981, 27:3.
72	16	Psalm 33:17, RSV.

Chapter 9. The Soviets

75	12	Sir Edward Grey, "25 Years: Battle of Britain July 10–October 31, 1940, 25th Anniversary," pamphlet (London: PRB Air, 1966).
76	12	E. P. Thompson and Dan Smith, eds., *Protest and Survive* (New York & London: Monthly Review Press, 1981).
76	31	Matthew 5:43–44, RSV.
77	5	William Butler Yeats, "The Stare's Nest by My Window," *Meditations in Time of Civil War,* VI, in *The Collected Poems of William Butler Yeats* (New York: Macmillan, 1957), pp. 202–203.
77	17	Quoted in Ronald Steel, "Cold War, Cold Comfort," *New Republic,* April 11, 1981, p. 15.
78	4	Numbers 14:18, KJV.
79	10	Matthew 7:1, KJV.
79	19	Casper Weinberger, speech to the American Newspaper Publishers Association conference, Washington, D.C., quoted in *New York Times,* May 6, 1981, 10:1.
82	22	Cyrus Vance, commencement address, Harvard University, Cambridge, Mass., 1980.

Chapter 10. Beating Burn-Out

87	2	Revelation 21:5, RSV.
87	11	2 Corinthians 4:16, RSV.
87	15	Edward the Confessor of England (d. 1066).
88	6	Isaiah 65:17, RSV.
90	10	Miguel de Unamuno, *Selected Works: Tragic Sense of Life in Men and Nations,* Vol. 4, ed. Anthony Kerrigan (Bollingen Series, Vol. 85) (Princeton, N.J.: Princeton University Press, 1968).
90	17	Samuel Beckett, *Waiting for Godot* (New York: Grove Press, 1954).

Index

Economics, 3–4; of the arms race, 81. *See also* Poverty; Wealth
Einstein, Albert, 72
El Salvador, 37, 78
Enemies, love of, 26–27, 77, 79
Etheredge, Lloyd, 71–72
Evil, hatred of, 89

Failure, 88; in love, 68; protective strategy of, 60–61
Falwell, Jerry, 41
Fear: choice of, 87; effects of, 9, 60; vs. love, 7, 11, 13, 60, 75; war induced by, 75–76

God, 2, 4, 7, 8; and abortion, 49–50; call of, 31–37; glory of, 12, 15; and individual development, 18; love of, 11, 13, 32, 36, 63; and the power of weakness, 27–28, 29; and renewal of hope for life, 87; and social responsibility, 32
Gomorrah, 42–43
Gratian, 51
Greed for personal salvation, 31, 59
Grey, Edward, 76

Hamilton, Alexander, 21
Hawthorne, Nathaniel, 1
Heine, Heinrich, 82
Homosexuality, 39–47; in the Bible, 42–43; Christian attitudes toward, 39–40, 43–46; theological approaches to, 41
Human unity, 62

Illness. *See* Sickness
Individuals, development of, 18–20
Innocence, 5–6; and abortion, 49–50
International income tax, 65
Irenaeus, 12
Israelites, 42; and the Promised Land, 59–60

Jesus Christ, 2, 3, 7, 22; conversion to, 32; death of, 21, 62; God's love incarnated by, 11, 14–15, 36;

on love of enemies, 77; and poverty, 4, 34, 63; and the story of the paralytic, 9–13 *passim*, 36; temptation of by the devil, 19, 68–69
Jewish-Christian relations, 45

Keen, Sam, 19–20
King, Martin Luther, 35, 37

Law of the Sea, 64
Levitical Code, 40, 41
Life: acceptance of personal limitations, 26–29; complete living of, 12, 15; human talents and aspirations for, 18–20; limits of, 17–29; of nations, 20–21, 88; pain in, 24, 26; suffering and grief in, 23–29 *passim*; survival of, 62; tragic aspects of, 20, 21. *See also* Abortion
Love: in the Christian Church, 36; courage for, 9–15; vs. dogma, 6, 8; of enemies, 26–27, 77, 79; failure in, 68; vs. fear, 7, 11, 13, 60, 75; of God, 11, 13, 32, 36, 63; importance of, 8, 35–36; joy of, 90; vs. rejection of homosexuality, 43–44

Manhattan, effects of a nuclear bomb on, 69–70
Marty, Martin, 5
Mary's Magnificat, 3, 63–64
Maslow, Abraham, 87
May, Rollo, 7
Mead, Margaret, 55
Meekness, 28
Michelangelo, 12, 39
Miller, Arthur, 24
Money, John, 44
Moralism, 2, 14
Moral Majority, 5–8, 88; political participation by, 6; preachers of, 5–6; problems of, 5–6, 87
Moses, 23, 60, 62; and the call of God, 31, 32–35, 37
Musste, A. J., 4

Nations: boundaries of, 63; com-

THREE PLAYS

THREE PLAYS

The Slot-Machine
The Interview
Pit Strike

Alan Sillitoe

W. H. ALLEN · LONDON
A Howard & Wyndham Company
1978

Printed and Bound in Great Britain by
Redwood Burn Ltd,
Trowbridge and Esher
for the Publishers, W. H. Allen & Co. Ltd,
44 Hill Street, London W1X 8LB

ISBN 0 491 02285 9

Contents

Preface

In the early summer of 1965 I went to stay with my brother in Shropshire. Our two families got into a car and cruised along lanes in the deep country to find a suitable spot in which to relax and, if possible, enjoy the scenery. We eventually parked the car and climbed a stile into a field.

There was something about this uneven carpet of green which stirred me so profoundly that I walked around it by myself and wrote on my notepad the idea for *The Slot-Machine*. If there was any part of England I wanted to own, I told myself, it was this. I imagined Woodstock and his family coming across it while on an outing from their gambling-machine workshop in Nottingham.

Woodstock climbed the stile and looked at the field with the same emotion as I did on first seeing it. The play is really about the ownership of land, and the way this issue affects the Woodstock clan. They decide to camp in the field overnight, and the ensuing clash with Lord Thoresby, the landowner, brings disaster on them all. The field has not been ripped apart for coal, as stated in the final act, and if ever I want to see it again I know exactly where to find it.

In working on *The Slot-Machine* I found myself having to deal with new problems. Being restricted to dialogue meant that the previous experience of writing prose helped very little. On the first page of the play people acted and spoke with far greater confidence than they ever would, it seemed, at the opening of a novel. From the beginning they were distinctly clothed and clearly featured. Set going by whatever I caused them to say, they then became intimidating in their demands for speech and action.

I was wary of being led where I might not have wanted to go, preferring to *move the pieces* only after giving my judgement the long time needed to reach proper decisions. I had an over-all plan, a theme, a theory or – at least – an idea. But once the startline was crossed – by Bernard Woodstock climbing the stile into the field – it was hard to keep things going at the leisurely pace and in the direction my idea required.

One can of course make minor cuts and additions when the first draft is done, though it is difficult to reshape the general design once it is basically out. The play emerged more harmonious and deadset than many a novel, a lockknit quality that made it feel so perilous to write, and hard to reshape once the premise was stated.

Real actors and actresses are eventually brought face to face with the people in the play. For a while they are quite distinct, but after a time (during rehearsals) both sides lose their abrasive antagonism towards each other. Before this ideal state is achieved it seems that the actors cannot possibly get close to the people I had created. They don't look like them, for a start, though they have been chosen to relate as nearly as possible. Again, they do not talk as I heard the characters speak when writing down their words. I was both exhilarated and embarrassed at having set such problems going.

But so diligent and skilful are the actors, that the original characters do eventually come to life and, hopefully, the curtain goes up. When it does the audience has to feel that it also is taking part in the play. I don't mean that they are pointedly invited to clap hands, answer back, or listen to insults showered on them from stage and

7

dress-circle, but that the combination of writer, director and, above all, actors, may influence them to feed back their enjoyment – and therefore their participation – to the actors who, in turn, are able to increase the effect of what they are doing.

By writing a play the author is merely the initiator of the *wonder-machine*, because he then hands it to a director, and actors who bring out the finer points of his characters in flesh and blood. With the novel, I observed, the people in it are less distinct at the beginning, and grow out of additional minutiae as the narrative goes forward, giving more control over the growth and movement. Unlike the playwright, who speaks to many people at the same time, the novelist reaches a single person who sees events in his individual way and creates a reality from the author's words inside his own mind. A novelist is a dictator whose words are final, whereas a playwright has to come to terms with a democracy – of sorts.

The first draft of *The Slot-Machine* was written in Karelia, mostly by the summer daylight of the midnight sun after everyone had left the hotel dining-room. Over the next five years it was polished and rewritten, and was performed (under the title *This Foreign Field*) at the Roundhouse in London by William Martin's Contemporary Theatre in 1970. Since then it has gone through many more changes, and is now called *The Slot-Machine*.

The Interview is of one act only, and concerns the plight of a woman in Russia – Irina Krichev – who wants to emigrate to Israel. I was asked to write it by the Women's Campaign For Soviet Jewry, and I can only hope that the play makes its point.

History teaches, and life often reinforces the fact, that a position has to be taken on the plain matter of human freedom. Those who are afflicted by the lack of it, who wait and endure, must find history meaningless, its importance being concealed by the humdrum daily happenings of their lives.

The most unlikely person occasionally becomes the representative of a collective spirit, and though I see Irina Krichev in this way I am sure she would prefer that her plight did not exist so that she could live a full, ordinary and indeed anonymous life. *The Interview* is simply concerned with her fate because she is not allowed to leave the country she was born in. To me, who can go anywhere, providing I have the time, the money or the energy, this is a basic and inhumane deprivation. One cannot therefore help but be affected by the harassment (and very real suffering) which, unfortunately, still goes on.

I wrote the play as if it were a transcript of an actual conversation between her and the emigration officer, much as if I had, for a change, been able to put a microphone behind a picture in the office where 'the interview' takes place – in other words, bugged the buggers instead of them bugging me.

After the play was put on I was accused in the Russian magazine *Sovietskaya Kultura* of being (among other things) in the hands of 'an international Zionist network of agents'. I never reply to *literary* criticism, but slander is different, especially from Russians who have been bitten by the mad-dog of anti-Zionism. The phrases they used showed that it is nothing less than anti-Semitism rearing its satanic head once more. In the rest of the world also, whether among the Extreme Right or the so-called Left, anti-Zionism has become the new anti-semitism.

The Interview was put on by Colin Blakely, Gerry Sundquist and Janet Suzman at St Martin-in-the-Fields on 16 September 1976. At the end of Janet Suzman's portrayal of the heroine (for such she is) one could only ask: 'For how long can I endure to see the evil that shall come unto my people? Or how can I endure to see the destruction of my kindred?'

A new performance, of an extended version of the play, was given for three weeks in March 1978 by the 'Almost Free' theatre, as a lunchtime production. On that occasion the actors were Diana Fairfax, Glyn Owen and John Rees. The designer was Norman Coates, and the director Jack Emery.

The third play, *Pit Strike*, was based on a story from my book *Men Women And Children*, and was put out as a TV play by the BBC on 22 September 1977, directed by Roger Bamford, and produced by Graham Benson.

Brewster Mason played Joshua, a Nottinghamshire coalminer who goes south during a miners' strike to help picket the Thames Valley power stations. He is a man who is never without his Bible. He does not claim to be religious, nor does he belong to any church, but whenever there is a spare moment he reads it, and is able to quote from it on occasion. It is, in fact, his main comfort in unfamiliar London. The play ends with his losing it, and perhaps a book never vanished in more peculiar circumstances.

Joshua is not a typical coalminer, however – I have never seen anyone yet whom I thought of as 'typical' of anything – but he is hardworking and independent and, to refer back to *The Interview*, one might easily wonder how such a man would be dealt with under a totalitarian system. There is no way of knowing, and in many ways I hope there never will be – as much for Joshua's sake as for mine and everyone else's.

Alan Sillitoe
8 March 1978
Wittersham, Kent

THE SLOT-MACHINE

A play in three acts

People

Bernard Woodstock	– slot-machine manufacturer
Mary Woodstock	– wife to Bernard
Paul **Ernest** } **Ben**	– sons to Mary and Bernard Woodstock
June Barnsley	– daughter to Mary and Bernard Woodstock
George Barnsley	– husband of June, Woodstock's son-in-law
Pat Bingham	– girlfriend of Ben Woodstock
Leonard Aslockton	– gamekeeper to Lord Thoresby
Lord Peter Thoresby	– landowner
Wally	– workman

THE SLOT-MACHINE
Act One

SCENE

A field in remote and rural Staffordshire, some time in the middle sixties. It is a peaceful, midsummer, perfectly English field, with the most enticing grass in the world. It is flanked by a wood. A stile leads into the field from rear-right.

The Woodstock Family is on holiday, touring the countryside in two large cars. They disembark at this point for lunch – the first stop since leaving Nottingham that morning.

There is a screech of brakes from the lane back stage. Then the noise of opening and shutting car-doors, shouts and laughter.

Enter Bernard Woodstock, carrying a lunch-hamper. He is a tall man, almost sixty, who holds himself well and looks around with confidence. His greying hair and regular features make his face appear rather too hard. He is wearing a suit, but no hat.

Woodstock puts the hamper down and sits for a moment on the stile, hands on knees set slightly apart.

Woodstock: Beautiful. Come and have a dekko at this, then.
Paul: *(off)* What?
Woodstock: This field. I never knew beauty had a smell to it.

Woodstock comes from the stile and into the field, setting the lunch-basket in the middle of it.

Enter Paul Woodstock. He is ginger-haired, and a stocky man for his age of twenty years – a cheerful person who might appear naïve and even ignorant to those who don't know him, but who certainly seems full of seriousness and sensibility to his inarticulate self. In fact to anyone with any perception he has a look of knowing far more than his twenty years. He is wearing a checked shirt and flannel trousers.

Paul climbs the fence, as if not noticing the easier way over the stile.

Paul: It's just like a million others.
Woodstock: Use the stile. You might injure yourself.
Paul: Fields are all the same to me, dad.
Woodstock: This one won't be if you damage your cobblers. You'll never forget it.
Paul: *(extricates himself well from the awkward position)* Are we going to eat our dinner here?
Woodstock: Might as well. We ain't had a bite since leaving Nottingham.

Enter George Barnsley, Woodstock's son-in-law, a man of about thirty – tall, thin, reliable. He is wearing a white shirt with rolled-up sleeves, and a tie fastened with a tie-pin. George never quite believes he has actually married into the Woodstock family, and behaves with diffidence, respect, and also the fear that he may one day be chucked out with not even the statutory notice that a normal factory-worker gets. Yet because he did, after all, marry into the family, he walks the tightrope of respect for it. In any case he is just a little too timid ever to show anything else.

George gets over the stile carrying two car blankets, a collapsible wash-basin and an orange plastic jerry-can of water. He sets up the wash-basin and pours water into it, then hangs a handtowel from the rail – all this being done while the others are coming on.

14

George then lays the blankets on the grass.

George: We ought to move the cars in a bit.

Woodstock: Go on! Nobody comes up that lane in a
  month o' Sundays.

George: They might, though, today.

*Woodstock takes off his jacket, rolls up his shirt-sleeves, and
washes his hands thoroughly.*

Woodstock: Let me worry about that.

George: Shall I go back to the car and get your hat?

Woodstock: No, don't bother. What do I want a bit o'
  cloth between me and God for? I want to feel the sweet
  air – every draught of it. Say what you like, Paul, but
  we ain't seen a field like this before. You don't need
  chairs to sit on, nor a table-cloth to eat from. Wait till
  your mother sees it.

George: The car might get knocked though, dad.

Woodstock: So will the other bloke's. It's good to get
  your hands washed. They get nearly as filthy driving a
  car as they do working a lathe.

Paul: It's a long time since you worked a lathe, dad.

Woodstock: I still know what it's like, though, don't I?

Paul: Well you ain't done it for a good while. That's all
  I'm saying.

Woodstock: All right, Paul. Just bloody-well calm down.
  Let this lovely English field soothe your nerves a bit.

*Enter June – née Woodstock, now married to George. She is
struggling to get over the perfectly simple stile. She is twenty-
four years old, middling in height, has a thin and vulnerable
face, rendered slightly pinched by a life-long effort to make her
way in the world of her family without being 'put upon'. She
is wearing a black skirt, white blouse brooched at the neck,
and high-heeled black shoes. She carries a suede handbag,
and a transistor radio.*

15

June: Why didn't you find a field with a gate to it, dad?

Paul: It's George – he wanted to see your knickers as you got over that thing.

June: Bollocks, you dirty-minded pig.

George: I can see 'em any time. We're married, aren't we?

June opens her handbag to check her face at the mirror inside. She does this now and again to make sure she's still there.

George: You're right, though, dad. Smell that air! There's no suds or swarf in that, Paul. A bit of lovely old England's good for the nerves! Ain't that right, love?

June: I'll tell you when I've had summat to eat. Why did you have to drive all this way without stopping once? Not even time for a pee.

Woodstock: Squat in that wood over there.

June: I don't want to pee.

Woodstock: What are you on about, then?

June: *(brings the heavy transistor radio across and sets it down by the lunch hamper)* I want to eat.

Woodstock: Well, bloody-well say so.

George: *(tipping water from collapsible handbasin and folding it up)* The others aren't here yet. We can't eat without them.

Woodstock: This is a perfect field. I told you we'd find one.

June: You never rest till you get exactly what you want, even though nobody else wants it.

George: We all wanted to find a nice field when we set out, love, you know that.

June: *(lighting a cigarette)* Who are you married to: him? Or me?

George: He's my father-in-law, ain't he?

Woodstock: *(takes a brandyflask out of his pocket)* Here y'are: burn a hole in your stomach with this while we wait. If I hadn't got what I wanted in life we wouldn't have a couple of good cars between us, and come on a holiday like this. Don't think it's going to be cheap, because it ain't. *(he passes the brandyflask to Paul)* I'm going to see where the others are.

George: You won't see much. That lane's as twisty as old Nick's bootlace.

Woodstock: Maybe they had a flat somewhere.

Exit Woodstock – neatly over the stile.

Paul: Old bastard.

June: Fancy saying that about your own father.

Paul: He's always been a mean old bastard as far as I'm concerned. The bullying old bastard.

June: Huh, the bickering's started. Whose idea was this trip, anyway?

George: We voted on it, remember?

June: You mean after that big booze-up for dad's birthday? If that's democracy you can stuff it, for export.

George: It's the nearest we'll get to it in this family. Let's have that three-star gripewater, Paul.

June: He as good as threatened to shut the brandy bottle if we didn't vote on his side.

From off-stage comes an alarming screech of brakes. Everyone freezes at the noise – George with the brandy halfway to his lips. He then drinks greedily, as if the others will take it from him when they arrive.

Woodstock: *(off: shouting above car doors slamming)* I'll *blind* you if you do that again.

George: What a way to greet your nearest and dearest.

June: Perhaps they bumped into him.

George: You'd better go and see, or he'll be on at us all day.

Woodstock: *(off)* You don't know how to treat a car, bladderhead!

Exit June – quickly.

Paul: If I hear his voice just once more I'll rip myself to
  bits.
Ernest: *(off)* You don't know how to park one.
George: I suppose I'd feel that way if I was his real son.
Woodstock: *(shouting: off)* If you've scratched the
  bodywork I'll stop it out of your wages.
Paul: *(doubling up as if from pain)* Oh God!
George: You ought to get married. Leave home.
Paul: I don't want to get married.
George: You ain't got much alternative, then.
Paul: I don't want to leave home, either.
George: Oh well, then.

*Enter Ernest Woodstock, over the stile, laden with two
cameras, a lightmeter and a pair of binoculars. Ernest is
twenty-eight, has fair wavy hair, and a moustache. A good
smile shows a set of expensive yet obvious false teeth. He
wears white flannels and a white shirt with a cravat at the
neck – and a naval sort of cap, jauntily. His lightweight
checked jacket is slung casually over his shoulders.*

Ernest: He parked on a bend as well. You'd think he
  owned the countryside.
George: I wonder who does, come to think of it?
Paul: We do.
George: You reckon so?
Paul: We're on it, aren't we? Let anybody try to shift us.
Ernest: That's what Ben says: all land should be owned by
  the people.
Paul: Yes, but he's a student, and he just talks about it.
George: When I was a young 'un I went out hiking in the
  country near Cotgrave. I leaned on a gate and it came
  off its hinges, so the farmer took me to court over it.
Paul: You should a gone back and burned his haystacks.
George: It was my fault, though. I reckon I knew what I

18

was doing: swinging on a gate like that without a thought in my head.

Ernest: What happened?

George: Got fined. Two quid.

Ernest: Two quid! Some people are born rotten.

George: Taught me a lesson, though.

Ernest: *(calling back)* Ben, Pat, throw them camp stools over. And that other basket.

Camp stools and other objects come sailing over, all neatly caught and passed on by Ernest.

Ernest: George, Paul, make a human chain, for God's sake.

No one attempts to co-operate and things go flying all over the place. Two folded stools narrowly miss George.

George: Hey, steady on. This is too much.

Paul: *(laughs)* Serves yer right for paying that fine.

Enter Mrs Mary Woodstock, a handsome but worn woman of fifty-five. She has tinted silver-blue hair and wears a pale blue summer coat and white shoes. She carries a large white handbag.

George: *(to Paul)* What's that got to do with it?

Enter Woodstock, gallantly helping his wife over the stile. He takes the gramophone from her.

Mrs Woodstock: What a *nice* field, Bernard. Look at them cows over there! They won't come near, though, will they?

Paul: We'll have some milk for us tea.

Mrs Woodstock: I've brought a bottle of pasteurised.

Enter behind her – Ben Woodstock, a son, a tall young man of twenty-two, student, wearing sweat-shirt and jeans.

Ben: (*a more normal neutral English accent*) Terrible stuff. It's bilge, not milk. We can afford proper milk, but you still get that.

Ben stands apart, opens a map and spies out the land with binoculars, marking marks on the map with a pencil as if planning military operations over it.

Mrs Woodstock: It don't spill in the car, that's why I got it. It *is* a lovely field.

Enter Pat Bingham, Ben's girlfriend, wearing a leather skirt, and a shirt, a BEA shoulder bag in one hand. She carries a huge bottle of champagne and a bag of ice.

Woodstock: Anyway, I'm glad *you* like it, Mary. Careful with that champagne, Pat. Put it over there. Don't drop the ice. We can't drink warm champagne.

Pat takes out a book and sits on a hump to read.

Enter June, struggling with a cardboard box.

Woodstock: And watch that box: it's got glasses in.
June: Give me a hand, then, somebody, or the cows'll have ground-glass for supper.
Mrs Woodstock: Just look at this mess already.
Ernest: I told 'em to catch. The only thing we do well is booze.
George: Now we've got to get it all straight.

Paul and Ernest spread the blankets. George opens and sets the chairs.

20

Woodstock: That's my lot, all over. It only takes 'em a minute to turn a field into a rubbish tip.

Woodstock walks up and down, inhaling and exhaling deeply.

Mrs Woodstock: Help me to get the food out, June.
June: All right, ma.

June and Mrs Woodstock arrange the picnic.

Ernest: Where's the crate of beer?
Pat: *(without looking up from her book)* There's nothing else in the cars except suitcases, and the tents.
Ernest: It was on my list.
Woodstock: You should have checked it.
Ernest: I did.
Woodstock: And checked it again. What's the point making a list unless you check it twice?
Ernest: I spend my bloody life making lists and ticking things off wi' a bit o' red pencil.
Woodstock: If I didn't insist on it we'd have bugger-all to check. Forgetting the beer!
George: We got the champagne, ain't we?
Woodstock: That's for a toast. We need something to *drink*. One of you had better go out foraging. Trust you to ruin our anniversary.
Ernest: I didn't mean to, dad.
Woodstock: You never do. You'll have to be a damned sight more efficient if you're ever going to run my business, though.
Ernest: I won't need to. You'll live for ever.
Woodstock: Stupid bloody fool.
Ben: *(still calmly looking at his map)* You'll come to a village two miles along the lane. Sedley, it's called. There's a pub, according to the map.
Ernest: Save me summat to eat.

Paul: If you hurry.

Ernest: *(shaking hands with Woodstock)* Goodbye, then.

Woodstock: Don't be long. My gut's rumbling.

Ernest: *(shaking hands with Mrs Woodstock)* See you later, ma.

Mrs Woodstock: Look after yourself, son.

Ernest: See you all, then.

George: Goodbye.

Ben: So long. Caio!

June: Tarr-ar.

Paul: See you.

Ernest: I'll be back.

Paul: I know you will.

June: You'll be all right, Ernie.

Ernest: See you in a bit, O.K.?

Exit Ernest – reluctantly, as if he might never come back.

Pat: Does he always say goodbye like that?

George: He's very hot on family feeling, Ernest is. He can't stand being on his own. We left him on his own once to look after the factory, and when we came back he'd got a hernia!

There is a noise from the lane, of a car starting up with desperate fervour.

Mrs Woodstock: I still don't think he's forgiven us for it.

George: He got a week in bed, though, in that posh private clinic.

Ben: Yes, and we had to take turns sitting with him twenty-four hours a day.

Paul: Even if he's going for a crap he kisses us goodbye, as if we'll never see him again.

Woodstock: It's just one of his bad habits, that's all. I tried to break him of it, but got fed up when I couldn't. I hate people who won't leave off their bad habits. It's

22

just a trick, I sometimes think, to turn you into a bully. Still, it's good to be on holiday.

June: It was better in Majorca.

Mrs Woodstock: I liked it when we went to Nice, Bernard.

Paul: Tangier was my favourite.

Ben: Yes. A camel fell in love with him.

Woodstock: Tangier, Nice, Majorca! You don't know when you're well off. Last year's trip to Benidorm cost me nine hundred pounds, and all I got for it was an olive walking stick to help my sprained ankle when I slipped on that rock. June got sunburn, George went down with a stiff dose of the gut-ache that sets him singing 'The Rock of Ages' when he can't stand it any longer, and Ernest was stung by a jellyfish on the hanging gardens of Babylon. We got back like a gang of walking wounded.

Pat: Ben and I hitch-hiked to Athens.

Woodstock: I know, but I tell you I'm fed up with such places. I want to see a bit of old England for a change. A few fields, a country pub or two, a thatched cottage, a winding stream, a bit of rolling woodland. Even a stately home: I don't mind. I haven't done such a jaunt for years. The doctor said I needed a rest.

Ben: The owls at midnight won't let us sleep.

Woodstock: But they'll be English owls, bless their hot little hearts.

Pat: I believe you're just a frustrated romantic, Mr Woodstock.

Woodstock: (*rather pleased at the idea*) Well, that's better than nothing. A frustrated romantic! You hear that, you lot?

Pat: Ben's a realist. On the way to Greece *I* carried the pack, and got us all the lifts. He lay in a ditch or behind a stone wall, while I argued to get both of us on the lorry.

Paul: Our Ben allus lets others do the work for him.

Ben: Wind back into your shell, Brawn.

Paul: All right, Brains. He can't even drive a car. Do you remember what we called him as kids, though?

Mrs Woodstock: It does upset me when you torment one another. Stop it.

Paul: Stand by. He'd just *stand by* when anything was going on, even at meal times. He wasn't weaned till he was fourteen. Came clobbering in from that posh grammar school and plugged on.

Mrs Woodstock: You'll be packed off home if you don't stop it. Ever since I started having you lot I've had a lump in my stomach, a pain in my heart, and a headache. If only I could have a bit of peace in my life. Now be quiet, and love one another for a change.

Paul: Can't even have a bit of fun now.

Mrs Woodstock: It's not fun, that sort of thing.

Ben: No, but it's insulting, and that's his idea of being working-class. Instead of believing in something intelligent like socialism.

Paul: I'm not working-class. You might be my brother, but you've got no right to say that. And you can stuff socialism up your arse.

Ben: What do you think you are, then? Nature's aristocrat?

June: Oh shut up, Ben.

Woodstock: I suppose standing on a muddy road in that Yugoslavian People's Paradise with the rain pouring down your neck made you feel good, did it?

Ben: Yes – at least I was in a communist country, and didn't have to listen to Paul's ravings.

Woodstock: Bloody-well pack it in, then. Come on, get a drink of this brandy everybody. Paul, Ben, you wouldn't spoil your dad's outing, would you? There's another thirteen days yet. If it's got to happen, save it till the end, when we're all fed-up and bilious, and doing a ton on the last lap of that dangerous road through the Pennines. *You* know the one: between

24

Matlock and Ambergate. That's the place for a real set-to. I can see it already. We'll meet some bloody fool in his little grey car, coming in the opposite direction, on the grey road with no lights on, at dusk in a teeming drizzle – just as we're overtaking a juggernaut on a bend. That's when we'll be having the biggest argument of the holiday. I know you lot, all right.

June: Don't, dad. You make my blood run cold.

Woodstock: You're lucky to have it running at all, duck. I wish mine was. But do you remember coming back on that jet from Majorca two years ago? It's something *I* never want to do again, not at eighteen thousand feet, anyway. June running to the lavatory with a black eye; your mother clouting me with the dinner tray; Ben and George having a savage punch-up near the emergency exit; Ernie and Paul trying to part 'em. The poor stewardess got the pilot to come and read the Riot Act. Threatened to land at Bordeaux and have us thrown into the galleys. We're all one family, Ben, no matter what class they told you we are at that university. Where the hell's Ernest got to?

June: *(drinking brandy)* Saying goodbye to everybody in the pub, I expect.

Ben: *(taking the brandy bottle from June)* If you've got good brandy it doesn't matter whose company you're in.

Woodstock: Aye, there's not much you can't get with money, Ben. Everybody defers to me, even though they call me a racketeer behind my back – because we make one-armed bandits in our workshop, and rent 'em out to pubs and clubs. It wasn't easy to build up my business. I go into the bank now, and it's 'Yes, Mr Woodstock.' 'No, Mr Woodstock.' Smiles all round, just because of money. They'd kick us aside like dogs if we didn't have money. I know the bastards more than you do.

Ben: I hate your money. You make it from selling gambling machines. One-armed bandits: the opium of the proletariat.

Woodstock: Opium be buggered. Money's money, and you've never been without it, that's why you can afford to hate it. I once knew a man who looked on money with contempt as well – used to talk about going to the bank to get another handful of those 'little crinkly bits of paper' – as if it was confetti God threw about on a sunny day. He joked about it so much that one day he didn't have any. Came and asked me to lend him 'a five-pound note'.

Pat: And did you?

Woodstock: Only once, my love. If I lost everything tomorrow I'd still be able to earn a living, because I'm a skilled mechanic.

Paul: You used to be.

Woodstock: Did I? Who invented that vertical switchback for bent pennies, then? *And* converted it to bent tanners after the war?

June: *You* did, dad.

Woodstock: *And* I've modified it for ten-pee pieces. Put in a dud and it spits in your eye. Been pirated all over the place. If I'd done it for a gunsight I'd be a hero drawing a pension. You know, I think I've been in this field before.

June: Why don't we pack up and go to Birmingham, then? It might rain soon. We can book in at a hotel, and go out to a dance. There's too many gnats and flies here.

Woodstock: Towns are out. If it rains we've got the tents. It's bloody familiar, this field is.

June: Let's vote on it, then.

Woodstock: We can't go changing our minds every minute.

June: I'm getting bitten to death.

Pat: I'm quite comfortable.

June: You would be, wouldn't you?

Ben: So am I. I've had enough of the car for one day. Even a field's more civilised than a car. Or it would be if it were owned by the people.

Paul: I wouldn't mind owning it.

Ben: I mean all the people.

Paul: What bloody good's that? I'm the people, aren't I?

Ben: You're only one of them.

Woodstock: Stop all this grumbling. You lot don't know you're born. When I was young life was hard. If you wanted anything you had to steal it. Nowadays all you've got to do is earn it.

Paul: You're allus on about the good old days.

Mrs Woodstock: I don't care what we do, as long as I don't have to get up and move.

Woodstock: They were bloody awful, but don't you dare say anything against them: I was young then. And they were marvellous as well. It's funny, though. It's as if I dreamed about this field. That gap in the hedge, the wood there. The land drops a bit on the other side, and there's a stream at the bottom. I'll bet a dollar on it. I'm going to have a look.

Exit Woodstock.

Paul: What's it like, mam, being married to a man of sixty?

Mrs Woodstock: He ain't sixty – till next April.

Ben: He talks too much, doesn't he? For another thing, he's too tall. The combination is fatal – for a bully.

Mrs Woodstock: That's why I married him. O not because he's a bully. You know where you stand with a talker. And at least it ain't dull.

Ben: You'll be telling us you had a hard struggle next.

Mrs Woodstock: You wouldn't understand if I did. And we *did*, let me tell you.

There is a piercing screech of brakes from the lane, signifying Ernest's return.

Mrs Woodstock: If I hear that pig-squeal of brakes again I'll have a heart-attack.

27

June: It makes me think of bad news.

George: It makes me want to run for it.

Paul: You can't run from this family. Ask Ernest. Even Ben can't. If he thinks being a communist will get him away from it he's even more bonkers than I am.

Enter Ernest.

Ernest: Get the chickens out; the prodigal son's come back. Where's dad?

George: Gone for a walk.

Ernest: At a time like this?

June: It's a slimming holiday. I'm bloody starving.

Mrs Woodstock: Is it a nice pub?

Ernest: A pub's a pub for all that. There's a telly in the bar. Even got a brace of dad's slot-machines in the snug. Our name's still on 'em.

Ben: There's fame for you. The height of achievement for a self-made man.

Pat: Oh shut up, Ben. You're always sniping.

George: Even your girlfriend's telling you off.

Ben: There's a lot to snipe at in this family. They're trying to be petit-bourgeois when they could be lords of creation!

Pat: You're part of the same lot.

The others turn to setting out the meal, and leave them to talk alone.

Ben: That's what you think. I'm no slot-machine mechanic. It's got 'student' in *my* passport.

June: *(overhearing)* Oooh! A bone-idle student throwing his weight about, eh? You're only poncing off us, you jumped-up dictionary. You'll have to do some proper work one day and then you'll come down to earth.

Ben: *(ignoring June)* They'll never forgive me for getting to university.

28

Pat: Why should they? I don't blame them, in a way. *My* family's like yours, but it doesn't bother me. Do you remember when we first met? I was fifteen, you were sixteen. My father had just got back from a Peace March, and wanted a slab of pork pie for his supper, so he sent me out. I wouldn't go at first, because he hadn't taken me with him, but when he promised to take me the next time I went. Then you got to university, and I made it to teachers training college, but that doesn't mean we've got to run away from our families.

Paul: He can run away from this one for all I care.

Ben: I can't stand being preached at. I'm not trying to run away from the family. I want to give it more dignity – under socialism.

Pat: Look, I'm a socialist as well, but I enjoyed coming here in the car this morning, being back among my own people for a change.

Ben: I know. But I believe that socialism, like charity, should begin at home. Or at least that it shouldn't be neglected. But can you imagine making any progress here?

Pat: Listen, we're on holiday, so let's relax.

Ben: I suppose we might as well. Do you remember how marvellous it was in Greece, on that beach near Corinth? We had food and a sleeping bag, and woke to the sound of the sea.

Pat: And you started reading Byron to me? You were funny!

Enter Woodstock, white-faced and shaken.

Woodstock: It *is* the same place.

Paul: What is, dad?

Woodstock: We used to come poaching round this way.

Ernest: You look stricken.

Woodstock: I'll be damned!

June: Let's eat, anyway.

Woodstock: I'll be *damned*, I say.

Mrs Woodstock: You've gone all white, Bernard.

George: (*opening shooting-stick*) Here, sit down.

Pat: (*pouring brandy*) Drink this, Mr Woodstock.

Woodstock: (*sitting down, and taking a drink*) I'd never have believed it. I thought I was in control of every sprocket of myself. I feel like a stupid kid, coming back to this place.

June: Let's pack up and go, then. This field don't thrill me, I can tell you.

Paul: There's millions like this.

Woodstock: (*giving the brandy bottle to Paul*) There aren't. Give me some of that chicken.

They forget Woodstock's troubles and begin to eat.

Paul: We ought to leave, though.

Woodstock: I'll have to think about it.

There is the sound of eating, and squabbling over choice pieces.

Mrs Woodstock: What about the toast, Bernard? You make all this fuss about our thirtieth anniversary, and then forget it.

George: She's right, dad: thirty years of medieval bliss.

Glasses are passed, a bottle handed over. The cork is eased off.

Woodstock: I'll show you how I love your mother still. Stop guzzling beer and drink some real stuff. You don't sup this out of a cup while you're smoking a pipe.

Mrs Woodstock: You always *have* loved me, Bernard.

Woodstock: I allus will, an' all. I know what love is, I do.

Paul: What is it, then, dad?

Woodstock: It's looking after your family. If you look

after your kids it proves you love your wife. Ain't that right, Mary? I like to see you all scoffing and guzzling, I do know that. Does any man's heart good! I don't care what you say about life in Russia, Ben, but this little scene 'ud tek some beating.

Ben: It used to be a chicken in every pot. Now it's a glass of champagne in every fist.

Woodstock: Eh? Look, if you don't stop them remarks, I'll punch you from here to bloody Stafford. Don't think you can get away with it just because you're my son. Have a bit more respect for your mother. They aren't teaching you manners at that university, and that's a fact.

Ben: You didn't send me there, and that's another fact. It didn't cost you a penny.

Woodstock: Listen, who paid the fine after you got arrested in that riot in Grosvenor Square? You wanted to go to prison for thirty days as a protest, didn't you, you bloody fool! But I went to the copshop and coughed up the money.

Ben: I'll never forgive you for it.

Woodstock: Nobody goes to clink in my family. I was there myself once and didn't want any son of mine to go through the same. If I'd known what I know now, though, you'd have been down a bloody coalmine at six years of age.

Mrs Woodstock: Stop it, both of you.

Ernest: Thank God *I'm* not class conscious.

Ben: You're not conscious at all.

Ernest: In my own way I am.

Paul: I'll go for him one of these days, and there won't be much left if I do.

Ben: Just because I can't lift a pintable in each hand don't think I can't break your head.

Woodstock: If they weren't all fighting among themselves I'd know they were sickening for summat. Come on, June's eating all the grub.

Mrs Woodstock: She isn't pregnant, is she, George?

Ernest: He wouldn't know.

George: What are you getting at me for?

Mrs Woodstock: We could always do with another young 'un running around.

Paul: Labour's short in the workshop.

Ernest: We'd need an extra hamper, though, on trips like this.

Paul: And a new car.

Ernest: A minibus, you mean.

June: If you don't stop, I'm walking off. We've got our bus fare.

George: Just because we haven't had any kids yet you'd like to get rid of me. It's bloody savage.

Woodstock: They're only having a bit o' fun, George.

June: You might at least give us something to eat and drink.

Woodstock: Right: here's to your mother, and another thirty years. The first ten were the worst, the second ten were better, but in the third ten you're too numb to notice. Come on, slosh it back. Let's have a bit of music.

The transistor is switched on, some pop song battering the sultry air. The field is littered with bottles, paper, food, scraps, cigarette-packets, and they are beginning to look as if knee-deep in it – as if they do own the field, in fact.

CURTAIN

SCENE: SAME, AFTER LUNCH.

The Woodstocks are sprawled around the blankets on which the remains of the meal still rest. A huge belch comes from one of the men – there is uncertainty as to who let it out.

Ben: Rotten guts.

Paul: It was Ernest. I can tell 'em all.

George: Got different notes, every one of 'em.

Mrs Woodstock: You ought to be ashamed, whoever it was.

June: It's like a pigsty.

Woodstock: You're all wrong: it was me. *(belches again)*

Paul: It worn't. It was me. *(belches also)*

Ben: It's like an identification parade. After a bit of murder, robbery or rapine in Nottingham all the police have to do is line up the suspects and tell them to belch. They'll soon know whether it's any of our lot or not.

Ernest: We do it in our sleep even. Ben can belch as well, though. Do you remember when you belched the first verse of 'The Red Flag' on May Day?

Ben: Get me out of this nightmare.

George: It's like a lovely dream, is this field.

Mrs Woodstock: Do you remember *your* dreams, Bernard?

Woodstock: Not me. I dream, though, Mary. But when I wake up I see them disappearing into the fog on the back of a pantechnicon. I've just got a bad memory, that's all.

Ernest: Except for fields.

Someone belches, but it lacks the fervour and clarity of their earlier efforts.

Ben: Coming for a walk, Pat?

Pat: Not yet.

Paul: Go on, Pat, or he'll cry.

Ben: You're all wind and piss.
Paul: *(laughs)* I'm one of the people, though.

Exit Ben.

Woodstock: It's a good job I don't want peace. Let's go for a stroll, mother.
Ernest: You'll need wirecutters in that wood.
Woodstock: I've got 'em. *(holds them up)* Bring the shooting-stick, Ernest. Look at the view: there's a stream goes down through the fields. I remember it. Come on.

Exit Woodstock, Mrs Woodstock and Ernest.

June: Shall *we* go and have a look?
George: *(standing)* Might as well.
June: If only you'd give a straight yes or no for once in your life.
George: I said yes, didn't I?
June: Come *on*, then.

Exit June and George.

Paul: You off, as well?
Pat: Too much champagne makes me sleepy.
Paul: You only had a bit.
Pat: It was enough.
Paul: Are you thinking?
Pat: I always am.
Paul: What about?
Pat: Nothing, really.
Paul: I'd never admit to that. I'm too ignorant.
Pat: So am I.
Paul: You've been to college, though.
Pat: You make me feel like a monster – with a book through my head.

34

Paul: That's Ben's fault. He's always rubbing in the difference. I sometimes say: 'Bring a nice posh piece home to tea from the university so's I can pull her up to bed.' And all he says is: 'Why should I?' I was too low for any of his friends. He has all the luck, picking up somebody like you.

Pat: We met in a beer-off.

Paul: At least he can *talk* to you.

Pat: 'Why should I?' What a bloody cheek. I've had the same upbringing as you.

Paul: You're educated, though. Your old man's a communist.

Pat: Not any more. He's decided to enjoy life.

Paul: Maybe Ben will one day – after we're all dead.

Pat: Don't be daft.

Paul: Give us a kiss.

Pat: What?

Paul: It won't lead any further.

Pat: Leave me alone, stupid.

Paul: Stupid? Nobody can take a machine to pieces as quick as me – *and* put it back together again. Even dad admits to that. When I was a kid he gave me an old slot-machine to play with! I was so little I could hardly pull the handle. I can lift one up with one hand now.

Pat: Why are you so proud of your strength?

Paul: It's an asset, though, ain't it?

Pat: If you've got nothing else.

Paul: I've got more than you think.

Pat: Tell me about yourself, then.

Paul: Why should I?

Pat: I want to know what you're like.

Paul: Give me a kiss first. There's nobody to see.

Pat: Don't you ever lose patience?

Paul: Not with somebody like you. I've loved you for a long time.

Pat: What, ever since Ben did?

Paul: Sharpshit!

Pat: Aren't you ashamed to spoil it between us?

Paul: I try not to.

Pat: So do I.

Paul: *(kisses her)* The country always makes me feel like this.

Pat: Like what?

Paul: Let's make coitus!

Pat: *(laughs)*

Paul: Ain't that your sort of word?

Pat: You *are* funny.

Paul: I'll knock you for six if you say that again.

Pat: Violent, as well.

Paul: I didn't mean it.

Pat: I like you.

Paul: Do you?

Pat: *(taking him by the hand)* Come on.

Paul: What?

Pat: Let's go into the wood.

Pat and Paul exit towards another part of the wood.

CURTAIN

SCENE: SAME, HALF AN HOUR LATER.

Woodstock: *(off)* I tell you it *is* the same place. I was never more certain.

Enter Woodstock and Mrs Woodstock

Mrs Woodstock: You should know, Bernard.

Enter Ernest.

Ernest: I can't believe it, dad.
Woodstock: I'm standing on the exact spot. One of the keepers shot my mate in the back with a twelve-bore, and the other dropped me in a flying tackle. They left my mate bleeding to death to chase after me.

Enter June.

June: (*sitting*) If I walk another inch, I'll die.
Woodstock: All so's I could do a month in quad. Not there. Over there.
June: What's the difference? My feet are crippled.

Enter George.

Woodstock: They dragged me off to the Hall, and the landowner went on bashing me in the face till he couldn't take another breath. He enjoyed it. I swear blind he did.
George: A criminal always returns to the scene of the crime!
Mrs Woodstock: Shut up, you fool. Bernard's upset.
Woodstock: It was no crime. I poached because I didn't know how else to get anything to eat. It taught me a lesson, because when I came out of prison I borrowed five pounds, bought a secondhand slot-machine, fixed it up and rented it out. Then I got some of the lads together to make sure none of the others tried to smash it. When I had plenty of money, it didn't matter at being on the shady side of the law now and again. Oh God, my backache! It's got me right here.
Ernest: Too much driving. I told you to let me take over.
Mrs Woodstock: Here, love?
Woodstock: They wouldn't have held *me* at the point of a gun. I'd have run, whether they shot me or no, and

they knew it. A bit lower. Left a bit. Up a bit. Right a bit. Now left a bit. That's it.

Ernest: But why did you come back here, dad?

Woodstock: Don't stop. Oooh! Pull the little bleeder out by the tail. How do I know? It was an accident.

Ernest: Some bloody accident.

Mrs Woodstock: Better?

Woodstock: A lot, yes.

Mrs Woodstock: I can allus find it.

Woodstock: I knew it was somewhere in Staffordshire, but I ain't thought about it for years.

June: You must a done, dad. We all think about things.

Woodstock: I didn't. I tell you.

June: I expect you was too busy making money.

Woodstock: I call it working. You don't remember the name and address of a nightmare, though. It even smells the same. That hedge's a bit thicker over there.

June: We've dawdled long enough. Let's go to Wales. We'll be there before it gets dark if we set off now.

Woodstock: What's the hurry? Got worms or something? I thought we all liked it here?

Ernest: Here's Paul – with lipstick all over his clock.

Enter Paul, with confidence. He wipes his face on his sleeve, however, at hearing Ernest's remark.

Ernest: His face is clean, but his hands are guilty.

Woodstock: That's my son!

Enter Pat.

Paul: There's no guilt where I come from. Pat and me are thinking of getting engaged, aren't we, duck?

Woodstock: Engaged? What *is* this? Musical chairs among the birds? What's happened to Ben? Have you chopped him up and buried him? I used to think life was simple.

Paul: I know your idea of simple: you pull a handle and money drops out.

Woodstock: Ah! It's not *my* money, though. It's somebody else's, and that's not so simple.

Ernest: What are you getting engaged for?

Pat: We want to.

George: When's the wedding?

Paul: Could be now – as far as I'm concerned.

Woodstock: What do you mean, now? Expecting the sky to drop on your back? *(to Pat)* You were going to wait a couple of years for Ben. Till he'd made the Revolution, I suppose.

Pat: With Paul, it's different.

Woodstock: You can say that again. Not that I'm against having a schoolteacher in the family. If things go on like this we'll be almost respectable.

Paul: You aren't going to palm me off any more with twenty pounds a week and my keep, though. Jack it up to fifty, or I join the Sproat mob.

Woodstock: For every week you've worked I'll give you ten pounds when you're spliced. I don't use anybody's sweated labour.

Paul: You should have given it to me as a right, not doled it out like charity.

Woodstock: I thought you wouldn't mind.

Paul: Well, I did.

Woodstock: You never said owt, though.

Enter Ben.

June: That was a long walk.

Ben: There's so much barbed wire. It's worse than the Western Front. Talk about England's green and pleasant land.

Mrs Woodstock: Look at his hands. They're all gashed. Ernest, run to the car for the first-aid kit.

Ernest: Somebody else can be company runner tomorrow. Goodbye, Ben.

Ben: *(with a wave of his injured hand)* Goodbye.
Ernest: Goodbye, Ma.
Mrs Woodstock: Ta-tar, love.
Ernest: Goodbye, Dad.
Woodstock: *(knocking Ernest's hand away)* Piss off!!!
Ernest: *All* right!

Exit Ernest.

Ben: I had to climb six fences to get near the big house.
A one-armed gamekeeper with a double-barrelled shot-
gun warned me off. But I gave him the slip and hid
behind the bushes in the garden. It's an enormous stone
house, Elizabethan, I think, a central hall jutting out
towards the drop of the hill at right angles to the façade,
banked up by mullioned windows.

Enter Ernest, carrying first-aid box.

Ernest: I hope the iodine hasn't gone off.
Paul: It was all right when George last tasted it.

Mrs Woodstock puts a clumsy bandage around Ben's hand.

Woodstock: You said at *right* angles to the façade?
Ben: As far as I could see.
Woodstock: That sounds like it.
Ben: There's loads of sculpture and ornament in the
gables and round the pilasters, as well as statues along
some of the walls.
Woodstock: It seemed smaller in them days.
Mrs Woodstock: There, Ben. I hope it don't fester.
Ben: Thank you, mother.
Woodstock: Come on, let's put the tents up. We've
driven enough for one day.
Pat: Paul and I could stay here for ever, couldn't we, love?
Ben: What's all this, then?

Paul: Me and Pat – we've clicked!

Ben: What do you mean?

Pat: Sorry, Ben. It was coming to an end, though, wasn't it?

Ben: Was it?

Mrs Woodstock: Don't take it so hard, Ben.

Ben: Bloody-hell! O God! I've seen all I want to see of this place. I vote we get out.

Woodstock: Me and your mam want to stay. Who else does?

George: I'm with you.

Woodstock: That's three-one.

June: I want to shift out of this muck-hole. Let's go to Liverpool.

Ernest: Count me in, dad.

Woodstock: Good lad, Ernest. Come on, I need two-thirds. Say yes, Paul, and there'll be a slap-up engagement party when we get back.

Paul: Yer – all right.

Woodstock: That's my two-thirds. Come on – Paul, George, Ernest, Ben – get them tents out of the car.

Exit Paul, George, Ben – Ben being first off.

June: You've never had your own way so much since we started voting on things. Whose idea was it in the first place?

Woodstock: Ben suggested it a couple of years ago, to stop us wiping each other off the face of the earth. He thought democracy would get us used to his ideas of communism. How daft can you be?

Enter Paul and George, struggling over the stile with a heavy tent.

Paul: They're like bloody great pigs.

George: They weigh a ton.

Woodstock: So they should. They're the latest brand new bungalow tents. Nothing but the best for us.

Paul and George struggle with it to the centre of the stage and begin to undo the enormous package.

Woodstock: Go and get the stove and kettle, June. We'll be wanting our tea soon.

Exit June.

June: *(off)* Mind my stockings, then!
Ernest: *(off)* Well, get out of the way.

Enter Ernest and Ben, manoeuvring the second tent.

Woodstock: We'll have our own village when all three are up. A canvas housing estate.

Exit George and Paul.

George: Let's get the other.

Paul goes to Pat, and they are mildly 'necking' at a corner of the stage. Ernest and Ben are trying to sort out the second tent, but the complexity of it defeats them.

Enter June with stove and kettle.

Mrs Woodstock: Ernest, go and fill the kettle at the stream.
Ernest: O.K. ma.

Exit Ernest.

Enter George and Paul with the third tent, over the stile.

Woodstock: What about finding the gramophone, Ben, and giving us the last side of Beethoven's Ninth?

Mrs Woodstock: That'll be lovely, Bernard.

Woodstock: Go on, Ben, it'll sound a treat in the open air while we're having our tea.

Ben: If you insist. There's not much else I'm good for.

Enter Ernest with kettle. He puts it on the stove.

Woodstock: I do insist. But cheer up, lad. Root in the boot and see if you can dig it out.

Ernest: I think we've come to the end of the boot except for a bit of old road map and a tow rope.

Exit Ben.

A man, Leonard Aslockton, stands for some seconds unobserved, looking at this strange camp, and listening. He is tall, with short grey hair, probably the same age as Woodstock but in a rather better state of preservation. He has no left arm, but a double-barrelled twelve-bore slopes down from the loop of his right arm. He wears black trousers and an old sports coat.

Paul: I don't like classified music, ma.

George: Classical. Neither do I.

Ernest: Pop music's more my style. Who's this?

Woodstock: What a lot of likes and dislikes. I think old-fashioned waltzes are what they really want.

Paul: Like you, you mean? Who's what?

Ernest: Him.

Aslockton: (*stepping slowly in*) You're trespassing.

Woodstock: Where did you drop from?

Aslockton: My usual patrol. You'd better get out.

Woodstock: Trespassing never entered my head.

Aslockton: Well you are. I've kicked the arses of older people than you before.

Ernest: Kick mine, and I'll do you in.

Aslockton: Trespassers plague my life.

Paul: What are you going to do, then, Wingy, clap hands for the coppers?

Aslockton: You wouldn't be the first poacher I'd shot at.

Paul: You don't frighten me with that tuppeny gun.

Enter Ben with armful of records.

Ben: He's the one I saw near the house. Capitalist landowner's lackey! Gave him the slip.

Aslockton: You didn't. I trailed you all the time. Watched you wash your cut hands at the stream.

Woodstock: You work for the Hall?

Aslockton: Since I was fourteen. My father before me. His father before him. You'd better break camp and push on.

June: You should have listened to me. We could a bin in Bristol by now.

Woodstock: Give him a drop of brandy, Ernest. And a cigar. You'll like these, gamekeeper. I can see you're a man of taste.

Aslockton: *(taking a tubed cigar from Ernest and putting it in his pocket. He speaks more politely)* Your car's blocking the road. My van'll never get through, not to mention the Rolls from the Hall.

Ernest: We're making ourselves felt. *(gives a glass of brandy to Aslockton)*

Aslockton: I'll get screamed at for two days if you don't run. Got a wife and four kids to think on, I have. *(takes the brandy down in one gulp)* Here's to your health, anyway! *(puts glass down on the grass)* VSOP, ain't it?

Woodstock: Courvoisier. Where did you lose that arm — if I'm not being personal?

Aslockton: In the war. Sniper got me in Tunisia. I got him at the same time. He died. I was twice his age, so it served him right. Young bastard. Don't like young bastards. Too cocky, these days.

Woodstock: When you got my mate, you had two arms.

44

Aslockton: I'm still a crackshot with one. *(he lifts the gun to show that he can hold it still and straight)* Killed a couple o' rabbits this morning.

Woodstock: Cool customer, aren't you?

Aslockton: *(he takes the cigar from his pocket. Ernest unpacks it and lights it for him)* A countryman, born and bred. The cigars are Cuban, I suppose?

Woodstock: Jamaican. Ever get this stuff from the squire?

Aslockton: You trying to be funny? Crate of beer at Christmas – if I'm at church. I'd still have two arms if it hadn't been for him. Came round when the last war started, saying as how every man-jack would be needed against the Germans. He allowed me half-wages while I was in khaki. He stayed behind. Chairman of the National Savings Committee. Colonel in the Home Guard. I look more maimed than I am, though.

Woodstock: You don't remember me?

Aslockton: All *you've* got to do is pack up and clear out. We don't like this sort o' thing around here.

Paul: Remember when I got that thug of the Sproats, dad? They was trying to take over our customers, so I fastened him against a wall and loosened every brick in it with his head.

Woodstock: Stop that, Paul. Hold back. I've no intention of clearing out, gamekeeper.

Aslockton: That's that, then, ain't it? You can't frighten me. I'm not that sort.

Woodstock: You can't frighten me. We're not that sort, either.

Aslockton: You'll have to go, though.

Woodstock: Do you remember one Sunday afternoon thirty years ago, when you shot a man in the back in this field? Where you're standing now? A young chap of twenty, had a wife and kid. Lay there bleeding to death, while you and another bloke sat on me. Died on his way to hospital.

Aslockton: Aye, there were one or two in them days, though he was the only one as died. It was every man for himself, if I remember rightly.

Paul: That sort of thing got you a long way, didn't it, Wingy?

Woodstock: Fill his glass, Ernest.

Aslockton: *(to Paul)* If you think my life's easy, I'll let fly at you. *(to Ernest)* Thanks. *(to Paul)* I never wanted to get anywhere. When you start work at fourteen you ain't got time to be ambitious.

Ben: Be quiet, Paul, or he'll rub another platitude in your face like a broken bottle.

Ernest: He's a bloody killer.

Aslockton: That chap's death was cleared up: misadventure.

Woodstock: Ever heard of Woodstock's Sportolas? You know: one-armed bandits? Slot-machines?

Aslockton: You've got more questions than a policeman. Cheers! *(belches)* I can tell it's Courvoisier.

Woodstock: Cheers!

Aslockton: Slot-machines? They're in every club and pub around here. Thoresby had 'em banned for a time, but he can't do much about 'em nowadays. You're Woodstock, then? I remember the name now.

Woodstock: It was my mate you killed. I never thought I'd bump into you like this.

Aslockton: It's finished, though.

Woodstock: Not if you think about it, it ain't.

Ben: What makes you so sure he can think?

Paul: Losing an arm should have helped.

Aslockton: What have you lost, then?

Woodstock: I lost my mate.

Aslockton: He was a poacher. It wasn't my fault.

Woodstock: It was *your* gun.

Aslockton: I lost the arm that pulled the trigger.

Woodstock: That wouldn't be any consolation to Jack Tibshelf. He'd rather still be here. I know he would.

46

Aslockton: You can argue as much as you like; I'm off to get help.

June: Me too.

George: Not with him, you're not.

June: He's jealous: I'll stay.

Aslockton: Listen, Lord Thoresby's got enough men at the House to make mincemeat of you lot. He's very touchy since his wife died. He'll have a bloody fit when he sees all this. The local coppers aren't very gentle, either.

Mrs Woodstock: *(filling kettle from stove)* Want a cup, gamekeeper?

Aslockton: No, I damned-well don't.

Paul: Don't insult my mother, maggot-head. *(he wrenches the gun free)* You one-armed murderer. *(he throws the gun to Ernest)*

Ernest: Don't move, or I'll blast you to bloody heaven and down again.

Paul: Not in the back, either.

Woodstock: Go easy with him, you two. I don't want anybody killed.

Mrs Woodstock: Be sensible, and have some tea, gamekeeper.

Paul: If he walks off, it *will* be in the back.

Mrs Woodstock: Pass the pastries, Ben. Everybody must be hungry in such lovely air.

George: Guests first.

Ben: Have one?

Aslockton snaps his arm at the box and it falls to the ground.

Mrs Woodstock: That sort of thing makes me ashamed of my own kind. They were the best cakes I could get.

George: He wants his gun.

Paul: You can have it, Wingy, if you beg for it – on your hands and knees.

Mrs Woodstock: Here's some tea.

Aslockton takes a cup.

Woodstock: Would you like a job in Nottingham, game-keeper? I could use a chap like you if ever you felt like a change. I like people who know their own mind.

Aslockton: *(putting his cup down)* Not bloody likely. *I* admire people who can be straight and honest, but there's not a bit of that among you lot. I shouldn't think you've ever heard such words. My father knocked 'em into me. Kicked me to Sunday School every week of my life. Bloody hard times, and I'll never forget 'em. Come on, give me that gun, and we'll say no more about it.

Paul: You'll never see that again, that lightweight double-barrelled twelve-bore for a one-armed murderer.

Aslockton: Lord Thoresby does his round of the estate at five. I'm on reconnaissance beforehand to see every-thing's shipshape. So I'm giving you fair warning. I regret having killed your mate. I nearly had to give up my job over it. But what's done's done.

Woodstock: I want to meet this Lord Thoresby again.

Aslockton: You wouldn't if you knew him like I do. He's been funny in the head lately, though he ain't seventy yet. His sort go like that. Too much port and pork. He lives hard compared to us. Never lets up. It's best to keep out of his way.

George: We ought to leave, dad.

Woodstock: No fear. I'm not the same man now as I was thirty years ago.

Mrs Woodstock: Aren't you, Bernard?

Woodstock: Maybe Ben's right, after all. Who can say who this land rightly belongs to? Go on, take a walk all of you, and look at the wonders of nature. If you can keep your traps shut when you get under them trees the silence might surprise you.

Ernest: I came here for a rest, not to play Cowboys and Indians.

Mrs Woodstock: You're trying to get rid of us, Bernard. You've allus wanted to get rid of us.

Aslockton: This tender scene's breaking my heart.

Paul: Leave my mother alone. If you aren't careful you'll lose your other arm.

Aslockton makes a sudden lunge at Paul, but does not hit him. Paul pushes him back, so that Aslockton bumps against Pat and sends her book flying.

Pat: Hey, leave me alone. *(she picks up her book)*

George holds Paul. Ben and Woodstock pinion Aslockton.

Mrs Woodstock: I'm not having it, Bernard. It's terrible. There's no peace anywhere. It's enough to break my heart.

Aslockton: I'll get you for this.

Paul: I'll pulverise *you*.

Mrs Woodstock: Who was it got Jack Tibshelf to go poaching thirty years ago? His mother heard you talking him into it that morning in the scullery. If it hadn't been for you he might have been here still. He'd never been poaching before.

Woodstock: That's a vile lie. On our anniversary you're trying to drag me down lower than a dog.

Mrs Woodstock: It's not a lie, and you know it. Things never go well when you start thinking of what happened years ago. You're not old enough for that sort of thing, Bernard. Jack Tibshelf would be here if it hadn't been for you.

Woodstock: Ay! Go on, rub it in till I'm bleeding from the face.

Aslockton: They've got us both in the dock now.

Ben: He wasn't born in it, like you.

Aslockton: You poor bastards: we were all born in it.

Ernest: *(throwing gun to Aslockton)* Take it.

Woodstock: *(to Aslockton)* Aye, perhaps we were. *(to the others)* Let's get them tents back in the cars. Maybe we'll find a hotel somewhere.

Enter Lord Thoresby. Middle height, sixtyish, balded and pear-shaped head. He has rather sensitive and troubled features. He is wearing plus-fours and a jacket, carries a double-barrelled shot-gun, and has a newspaper sticking from his pocket. He talks in a normal voice, but gets shriller and more threatening as the act closes.

Thoresby: Whose are those cars blocking the lane?

Aslockton: Good afternoon, Lord Thoresby.

Woodstock: Ours. We're resting up a bit.

Thoresby: If anyone's ill, there's a doctor in the village. You can park on the road, at a pinch, but picnicking and putting up tents is not allowed.

Woodstock: *(hand held out)* Woodstock's my name. Bernard Woodstock.

Thoresby: You'd better think up a good story, Aslockton. Things have been going to pieces lately.

Aslockton: They were here when I came, sir.

Thoresby: If they're friends of yours you can tell them to go. You fill your pockets by selling my fruit. Oh yes, I know you do. You even hawk my flowers and game in the village, and I've turned a blind eye to it for years, but I'm hanged if I'm going to put up with this.

Aslockton: But I told them to go.

Thoresby: Don't argue with *me!*

Mrs Woodstock: Give him some brandy, Ernest. He's upset.

Thoresby: *(shakes Woodstock's hand – briefly)* I'm Lord Thoresby. You happen to be on my land. Now let's have you off it.

June: You ought to keep your flies in order.

George: They get on her nerves.

50

Ernest: (*pushing their belongings together*) Let's get out of this.

Paul: And she scratched her drawers on the barbed-wire, mate.

Ben: Curb your dirty thoughts, can't you?

Thoresby: I can barely understand what they're saying.

Aslockton: I'll interpret, sir.

Ben: Keep calm, Paul. If you lose your temper you only play into their hands.

Thoresby: I can understand him, of course.

Paul: Back me up, Ben. We're on the same side.

Ben: Maybe. But it's no use being sentimental about it. You have to think this through, and plan it properly.

Paul: You're a coward. Where's all your revolution stuff now, then?

Ben: You're barmy. You need intelligence and discipline.

Paul: My bloody arse, you do!

Woodstock: Pack it in, you two.

Thoresby: Are they quarrelling?

Aslockton: They don't do much else, sir.

Thoresby: Scum of the earth, eh?

Aslockton: They are, sir. Worse.

Paul: I can't stand it.

Mrs Woodstock: Let me tell you what you was like as a little boy, Paul.

Paul: We're on our own land.

Aslockton: Are you!

Mrs Woodstock: You were the gentlest boy I had. You sat in the kitchen for hours playing with a piece of old machinery.

Paul: A bomb's ticking. But my feet are on the earth. The earth's mine!

Mrs Woodstock: And when I went out of the room you were all upset. You were a gentle and patient child.

Paul: If you stab me, I'll bleed soil. Shoot me, and mushrooms will die. It's our land. I want this field.

Thoresby: The fellow's ill. I've seen it before.

Mrs Woodstock: Ben was the wild one. Used to smash everything. And now look at him.

Paul: They want to exterminate us.

Thoresby: I'd get him to a doctor if I were you.

Paul: You won't kill us off, you bastard.

Aslockton: Speak civil to Lord Thoresby.

Thoresby: They're from Derby, I suppose?

Aslockton: Nottingham, sir.

Thoresby: Ah!

Paul: Come on, dad. Let's get 'im, Ernie. Come on.

Thoresby: Any violence, and I fire. Get those tents away from here, or I send for the police. I'll have no more of this. I've nothing against you, but you're spoiling my land. It hurts me even to see someone walking across it. I own it. I'm not boasting. I only state a fact. I never thought I'd see such rubbish on my beautiful field.

Ernest: It's no good, Paul.

Woodstock: Let's go, then. *That's an order.*

George, Ben, and Ernest begin collecting their belongings.

Paul: Don't touch 'em.

Pat: We must go, Paul.

Paul: I won't.

Pat: Don't be stupid.

Paul walks a few steps towards Thoresby. Thoresby advances with gun level.

Thoresby: Get off my field.

Paul: There's . . . I've nowt to lose.

Thoresby fires the gun – once. Mrs Woodstock screams. The second barrel is fired.

Pat: Paul!

CURTAIN

Act Two

SCENE: TEN DAYS LATER.

The Interior of a large bungalow tent set in the same field.

Thoresby, Woodstock, Aslockton, and Ben are sitting around a card table. A lamp hangs above the middle of it, illuminating a plan of the estate spread over the green cloth. Two camp beds to the side.

Ben: As far as I'm concerned, the hour of reckoning is at hand.

Woodstock: The Revolution's begun, Thoresby!

Thoresby: We made an agreement. On the spur of the moment.

Ben: To save your neck.

Woodstock: You didn't shoot my son on the spur of the moment. It was premeditated murder.

Thoresby: I'll stand by what I said.

Woodstock: So will we. In spite of our loss.

Thoresby: This is the most tragic night of my life.

Ben: Oh, if only you'd say something real – so that if anyone asks what you're like I'll be able to tell them.

Woodstock: Be quiet, Ben. *We* understand each other.

Thoresby: I've never had any difficulty in feeling real – until now.

Ben: Nor me. I've had enough of this field. I've never known soil to *stink* so much.

Woodstock: You'd better get used to it. We own it, and twenty others, from now on. We're coming into our birthright. Isn't that what you allus wanted – for the land to belong to the people? Ah-ah-ah-ah!

Thoresby: If I may put in a word.

Woodstock: *(shouts)* We're *amicable*.

Ben: I'm not. Nor is Paul's dead body.

Woodstock: Calm down, Ben. It's always over *some* dead body. There's nothing we can do about it now.

Ben: It's too dark in here.

Woodstock: Turn the wick up, then.

Ben: It's full on already.

Woodstock: Root out the other lamp.

Ben: That's no good, either.

Woodstock: We'll have to buy more powerful ones.

Ben: They don't exist.

Woodstock: You remember those at that Swedish exhibition? Cure anybody's blindness. What was I saying?

Ben: About the land.

Woodstock: Oh yes. Thoresby! What about it?

Thoresby: You can have the area agreed on, but not this field. I can't tell you how fond I am of it. It will be like cutting off my own foot.

Woodstock: I'm not forgetting my place when I say this, but you fired that gun in cold blood – both barrels.

Ben: With a long premeditated interval between each shot.

Thoresby: You were trespassing.

Woodstock: I didn't see a notice board.

Thoresby: But I told you. So did my keeper.

Aslockton: True, Mr Woodstock.

Woodstock: Shurrup, bandit. We were packing up to go. You murdered Paul in cold blood, Thoresby, and every one of us saw you. You were so calm, that I'll get you to stick to the letter of our agreement.

Thoresby: We made it rather quickly.

Woodstock: To save your neck.

Ben: The inquest went like clockwork. Thanks to us.

Woodstock: Death by misadventure!

Ben: You should be in jail for the next thirty years.

Woodstock: What good would that do? He'd be rotting, and we'd get no land.

Ben: I don't want his land.

Woodstock: You did, though, didn't you?

Ben: That's all finished with now.

Woodstock: Is it, then? Paul would have wanted it. I can see him now, my own proud son striding about on it as if he'd live for ever. *(to Thoresby)* I'll have every blade of grass, every nettle and bush, every drop of your blood for this. My grief hasn't started yet. When it does, I'll skin you alive. I can feel the icebergs waiting to break through. You promised me a third of this estate.

Thoresby: Everything will be signed over in the morning.

Woodstock: It'd better be.

Ben: What will we do with so much land?

Woodstock: I'll settle that when I come to it. But it'll be your problem as well when I've gone over the hill, Ben, my boy!

Ben: I don't want it.

Woodstock: You will.

Ben: When I think of Paul, I can't go on living.

Woodstock: Can't you? Do you remember that argument you had with Ernest last Christmas about socialism – when we were all on the beach in the Canary Islands knocking off tots of whisky—? You said you can't make an omelette without breaking eggs. It seemed stupid and cruel to me then to say such a thing, but I see what you mean now, because it's a case of having to. Paul was the egg that had to be broken. But our hearts are broken as well, and that being so – don't you see? – we might as well get some advantage from it. It won't mend our hearts. It never will. But somebody's got to pay for his death.

Thoresby: I am sorry about all this.

Woodstock: We all are. We sympathise with *you* in *your* loss. I'll turn your estate into a desert. I'll plough it with salt. I'll sell it off plot by plot and scatter it with a poxy rash of pink matchbox bungalows, so that every time you open a window from the big house or step out for a breath of air you'll be face to face with a woman in curlers emptying dinner scraps into a dustbin. The sight of what I'll do with Paul's land will break your heart.

Thoresby: You won't get it. I'll hang myself.

Woodstock: (*gets Thoresby by the shoulders and pushes him back into the chair*) You–murdered–my–son!

Thoresby: And you perjured yourselves.

Thoresby gets up and stands by the entrance to the tent.

Woodstock: It was a gentleman's agreement. If we swore the gun went off accidentally in Paul's hands you'd give me a third of your estate.

Thoresby: I was at my wits' end.

Ben: That's a lie.

Woodstock: You broke down and slobbered all over us. I expected better from someone like you, but wonders'll never cease, I thought. You agreed to it the next day as well. But if that's what a gentleman's agreement means, I won't bloody own it.

Thoresby: I want some air. (*he steps outside*)

Woodstock: (*calls to him*) Take all you like. It's free. *That* belongs to both of us – at the moment.

Ben: He'll go back on his word.

Woodstock: (*standing up and walking across the tent*) He won't. We've had this out twenty times already. (*stops, suddenly*) Oh, my back's at it again.

Ben: You were sitting down too long.

Woodstock: That must be it.

Ben: Get him to sign this interim agreement.

Woodstock: It's gone.

Ben: He *can't* go back on it, then.

Woodstock: I've got my pride. If it's not held till

56

tomorrow, as a gentleman's agreement should be, I don't want it. I'm his bloody equal any day. He'll stick to it, mark my word.

Ben: He won't. His class never does.

Woodstock: We've got to trust him. It'll be all right.

Ben: I always thought you were a good business man.

Woodstock: (*sitting down at the table*) But there's pride, as well. That bloody animal's done too much damage. He's not going to treat *us* like shit any more.

Thoresby comes back into the tent, walks to the table, and sits down.

Thoresby: Let's discuss it like grown-up people.

Woodstock: Willingly.

Thoresby: Imagine we're in the army.

Woodstock: Pretend we're in court.

Ben: It's the revolution, Thoresby.

Woodstock: Stop that bloody stuff.

Thoresby: It's my land you're on.

Woodstock: It'll soon be mine. Resign yourself to it.

Thoresby: I damned-well won't.

Woodstock: Now we're talking like equals. We owe at least that much to Paul. Gone to sleep, gamekeeper?

Aslockton: I haven't slept for days.

Woodstock: Think you're going to get off scot-free, do you?

Aslockton: It's nothing to do with me. (*picks up the map from the table and looks vacantly at it*)

Woodstock: What are you here for, then? To carry Thoresby home when we've bled him dry?

Thoresby: Let's get this matter finished. We all have our dignity, and I have as much as anyone.

Woodstock: Have you? But I've got Paul's dignity on my shoulders, and Paul's dead, and Paul's dignity weighs a ton. (*he grabs the map from Aslockton and draws a line decisively across it in thick pencil*) My land is on this side

57

of the line, *(makes a great cross over it)* and yours is on *that* side. *(makes a smaller cross)*

Thoresby: But it crosses the river.

Woodstock: I'll block the river. Then you'll have floods to worry about as well.

Thoresby: It goes through the middle of the Hall.

Woodstock: Demolish the Hall, then it won't.

Thoresby: It's a historic residence. It's got a whole page in *The Buildings of England*.

Woodstock: Now it'll only have half. That side – all yours. This side – mine. I'm adamant where human rights are concerned.

Thoresby: You want *all* my land!

Woodstock: You mean all *my* land. I'm a broken man, Thoresby. My spirit's gone. I'm lower than the lowest snake on the earth. There's nothing you can do to me, so I'll get everything from you. You–killed–my–son! But I won't be vicious. I'll only take half.

Thoresby: The agreement was for a third.

Woodstock: Half.

Thoresby: We'll discuss it further.

Woodstock: You wouldn't get better terms anywhere.

Thoresby: Let's talk about it.

Woodstock: *(waves the map in the air)* Do you hear what I'm doing, Paul?

Thoresby: Half, then.

Woodstock: Settled. What good would all of it be to us? I'll want to see your blue nose now and again over the barbed wire. Have you ever seen a man before who's lost his son? Who wasn't wearing a uniform, I mean? I saw Jack Tibshelf's father when I got out of prison, gamekeeper. You shot him in the back for a couple of paltry rabbits. In those days we used to sell 'em for a shilling each.

Ben: Killing Paul blotted out Jack Tibshelf's murder.

Aslockton: *I* didn't murder him.

Woodstock: It'll blot us all out if we're not careful.

Thoresby: What do you mean? Blot who out?

Woodstock: What do you mean 'what do I mean'?

Thoresby: I want to understand, Woodstock.

Woodstock: Want to understand, do yer? You *have* come down in the world. But don't let it upset you!

Thoresby: How can a man be so despicable as to trade on the death of his own son?

Ben: You're trying to trap us. I don't like metaphysical questions, Thoresby.

Thoresby: It isn't a metaphysical question. It's a moral one.

Ben: In which case you haven't got a leg to stand on. If it's metaphysical it's irrelevant. If it's moral you're done for.

Woodstock: *(rubbing his hands)* There's nothing better than a good argument.

Thoresby: Universal education's an abominable thing.

Ben: Yes, you lot couldn't wriggle out of that one, could you? Had to teach us to read all those notices saying 'Trespassers Will Be Prosecuted'. A lot o' people ignored 'em, though, didn't they? Who fixes the boundaries, dad?

Woodstock: We do. But let's discuss the celebrations first.

Thoresby: What kind of celebrations?

Woodstock: We haven't made up our minds yet. Maybe a breakfast of champagne and fishcakes followed by massed brass bands and a firework display. Then a pop group to round off the morning. Or we could have non-stop Bingo in the bosky dell, backed-up by an afternoon booze-up between the tents and trees, ending in an archery competition, with an orgy at night for the youngsters. We might have an egg-and-spoon race through the spinneys, and a few rounds of skittles, if nobody minds.

Thoresby: I thought for such good land there be . . .

Woodstock: Something better? Paul's buried in the

village churchyard, eating God's earth, Thoresby. It's better to celebrate here than in Nottingham, so you bet we'll do it in style. Where you die, that's where you belong, it strikes me. Come on in then, Pat, and get the sky off your back!

Enter Pat, who has been standing just outside the tent. She is dressed in black.

Woodstock: Where's the others?

Ben: George drove them to Stafford for a night out.

Pat: Have you done haggling over your few blades of grass?

Ben: Why don't you stop acting the black widow? You should have gone back to Nottingham after the funeral.

Thoresby: Is there no respect for the girl's grief?

Woodstock: Shut up, you. That's not your department.

Ben: *(to Pat)* You only knew each other for half an hour in the wood.

Pat: He was your brother, and you still don't care about him.

Thoresby: They want their revenge on me, I'm afraid. I don't know what I've done.

Woodstock: You've done everything, Thoresby. But it's not revenge. It's just a matter of right and wrong.

Thoresby: I am to blame. I admit that.

Woodstock: Now you're talking sense.

Pat: We're all to blame. But nobody else here will admit it: what the Woodstocks want they get.

Woodstock: And a fat bloody lot we've got in the world, if you reckon it up.

Pat: You haven't got Paul any more. But you never wanted him, so you don't even know you've lost him.

Woodstock: Quiet!

Pat: I loved him.

Woodstock: That's because he's dead.

Ben: She used to love me. Or she said she did.

Pat: I hate you now.

Ben: You talk about what the Woodstocks want, but you don't know what *I* want any more. But I'll tell you: I want everything suddenly – though it's like wanting nothing, in the end. It's certainly the way to get nothing.

Pat: You can't show sorrow for Paul till you know what you want; and if you don't know what you want you can't lose anything you'd ever feel sorrow about.

Pat comes towards Ben, as if to comfort him.

Ben: Go away. Leave us alone.

Pat: I won't. I'll go back when the family go.

Thoresby: Come and stay at the Hall. You'll be taken care of there.

Ben: You're interfering in what doesn't concern you, Thoresby.

Thoresby: I'd like to help.

Ben: You don't belong with us.

Thoresby: You're right: I don't.

Woodstock: *(genially)* Calm down, everybody. As soon as we've got the land we'll go back to Nottingham for a spell. Get the profits rolling in again. That's more my line! I feel as if I've doubled the length of my life.

Pat: You've halved it by losing a son.

Woodstock: Do you think grief has to be seen to be believed? Everybody suffers in their own way. You can't be upset if you can be so sarcastic. So bloody-well stop it.

Thoresby: *(standing)* Come on, Aslockton. Let's put an end to this.

Woodstock: Where are you going?

Thoresby: To get some sleep.

Woodstock: You don't mind if I call you Peter, do you, Thoresby?

Thoresby: No. A long sleep.

Woodstock: Why don't you kip down here for the night, Peter?

Thoresby: I'd rather not.

Woodstock: Anyway, we're in accord.

Thoresby: Gentleman's agreement. *(to Pat)* I can't tell you how sorry I am.

Woodstock: *(slapping him on the back like an old friend)* No regrets, Peter. What's done's done.

Thoresby: *(to Pat)* You loved him, didn't you?

Pat: Yes.

Thoresby: *(to Woodstock)* Tomorrow, at ten.

Woodstock: We'll be there.

Thoresby: *(holds out his hand to Pat)* See me to my car, my dear.

Exit Pat and Thoresby, followed by Aslockton.

Ben: I kept wanting to kill him. I don't trust him. Nor her.

Woodstock: She'll be back. Don't think he'll get off with only half his land. I'll mortgage mine to buy his dirt-cheap when he can no longer stand the sight of us.

Ben: He shot Paul like a dog. Yet Thoresby's right: we're trading that for a slice of land. It's no good now that Paul's dead, anyway.

Woodstock: *You* didn't get on very well with him, so what the bloody-hell are you moaning about?

Ben: He was my brother, though. Hasn't this field had enough blood?

Woodstock: What's the difference? Every field's been saturated in it. *(holding Ben)* Stiffen up a bit. Get some of this brandy. In times of adversity we stand united. You're too young to remember that time after the War. The Sproats came out of it strong, but so did I. It was a matter of who was to be top dog. The fight lasted months, gang against gang, bribery, threats, the odd accident to either side. Time and again I thought I was beaten and lay down ready to give in. 'Die, Charlie,' I said to myself. 'Die, then!' But whenever I did I knew Sproat was saying the same. So I got up and plotted more moves. Your mother thought I had a headache that wouldn't heal. Near the end I chased Sproat through Town. What a car chase that was! He jumped the traffic lights at Chapel Bar. So did I. Spun through Slab Square. I spun after him. Then he shot down Wheeler Gate. I squealed on his tail. I cornered him at the back end of Broad Marsh. Pulled everything out of his van and scattered it all over the road. By the time we'd done you couldn't tell the difference between a one-armed bandit and a shot-down Spitfire engine.

Ben: It's a wonder the coppers didn't get you: speeding through Town like that.

Woodstock: Your mother thought of that before I set out. She helped me a lot.

Ben: How?

Woodstock: *(laughing)* She put a big notice on the back of my car saying JUST MARRIED! She's got a brain, don't forget, your mother has. We all pulled our weight in them days. What a time it was! I wish I had it to go through again, though.

Woodstock stops talking and stands stock still, a look of bewilderment and pain on his face.

Woodstock: Oh God!

Ben: Your back playing up?

Woodstock: One minute I can hardly feel it, the next it aches like hell.

Ben: You'll have to get it seen to.

Woodstock stands rubbing it a moment or two, looking abstractedly.

Woodstock: Fight, fight, fight – all the time. Then one morning Sproat came to see me, and by the look on

63

his face I knew it was over. He was under the front wheel of my steam-roller. *(he laughs. There is the sound of a motorhorn, and a crushing-in of car brakes from the lane)* Like Thoresby. He's not as strong as we are. He didn't need to give *us* anything. He cracked. He bled at the arse. I kept firm. Never forget it. My heart will deal with Paul when it's good and ready. Oh God, it's not far off, though. Come on, Ben, smile: here's the others.

Enter Mrs Woodstock and June.

Mrs Woodstock: He's a madhead. What's got into him? He drove back like Ned Ludd himself.
June: I told him not to drink whisky. He's used to brandy. It don't do to mix drinks.
Mrs Woodstock: I thought we'd be killed stone dead.
Woodstock: Picture good, darling?
Mrs Woodstock: We walked out halfway through. I can't keep my mind on anything.
Ben: *(drinking from the brandy bottle)* You need glasses, mam.
June: *(to Ben)* Don't glutton it. Pour me some.
Ben: I'm sorry.

Enter Ernest and George.

George: That car wants servicing.
Ernest: Steering's not so good, dad.
Woodstock: Tek it in tomorrow. We'll go to Stafford in the other.
Ernest: That's not so good, either.
Woodstock: Yes, things happen all at once.
George: Let's have a drink.
Woodstock: It'll do, though.
June: *(to George)* Careful, love. You'll have a blackout if you drink brandy.

Woodstock: If I drive we'll get there.

George: *(to June)* That's what I want: so's I won't hear your voice for twenty-four hours.

Ernest: After this little lot I'd get a chauffeur, if I was you, dad.

June: *(to George)* I don't like it when you come out of your shell.

Woodstock: When I can no longer sit at a steering wheel I'll be dead.

George: *(to June)* When I'm in it you think I'm a weakling.

Ernest: If that's how you feel.

June: Either way, it's not bloody pretty.

Ernest: Those two were snogging like a courting couple in the pictures, but as soon as we get back here the bickering starts. When are we going home, dad?

Woodstock: As soon as I've signed them papers.

Ernest: I wonder how our machines are getting on? I hope Wally's kept 'em oiled and polished. It'll tek a day or two to get the little darlings back to life, though. I'm sure orders and trouble have been piling up. Where's Pat?

Ben: Sobbing outside, I expect.

Mrs Woodstock: I'll be glad to sit at home again, and think about Paul. Nothing seems real out here.

Woodstock: Never mind, love. We've got land now! Land!

Ben: The Revolution's come home to roost all right.

Woodstock: Everything does. That's summat else you can't learn at University.

Mrs Woodstock: A few measly fields. All this heartache for a bit of land. And all you can say is: Never mind! This pain under my heart won't leave me. I've cried so much I can't even cry. If only you could help me.

Woodstock: My love!

Enter Pat, who stands silently apart, hardly noticed.

Mrs Woodstock: I know you can't, Bernard, so it's no use trying. What did you say when your pal was shot here, all those years ago?

Woodstock: Not a word. I sat in jail and burned to a cinder. Those brick walls bleached me dry. When I finished my time I felt like a scarecrow out of the kiln. I just wanted my own back. Thoresby's right. He's no fool. It *is* revenge. But I was young then, and I didn't let it bother me.

Mrs Woodstock: Your own son had to get killed, though.

Woodstock: If only it had been me.

Mrs Woodstock: But it wasn't, was it?

June: It ain't his fault, mam. He didn't kill him.

Woodstock: It *isn't* revenge. That's a bloody lie! I can't stand to think about Paul. It was Thoresby who spouted about revenge, to stop my hands ripping his windpipe out. But I'll have his land. I'll have him for it.

Pat: When Paul and I went into the wood I never thought he'd die so soon afterwards. When you're in love you think you're going to live for ever.

Mrs Woodstock: I wish I was drunk.

Woodstock: It was my fault.

Pat: You're feeling guilty *now*.

Woodstock: Do you want me to cut my throat?

Pat: Prove you loved him, and give up all this.

Woodstock: I did love him, but I can't.

Ben: *(to Pat)* Paul was violent with Thoresby because you drove him to it. He was always rough, but never suicidal – until you came into it.

Pat: All you could do was talk about Revolution, but Paul had the guts to get out in front and do something.

Woodstock: We'll have a Memorial Day every year. Paul won't be forgotten. We'll straighten the land so's you can see it a mile off, and build a great monument. I'll spend thousands. Ben can get some famous poem chiselled on it.

Pat: You're not only callous, you're going crazy.

Ben: We'll both own this land one day, if you marry me.

June: Keep your grab-alling ideas to yourself. It'll belong to me and George.

Woodstock: I'll decide who it's going to.

Pat: Give it up. You're stealing it from Thoresby.

Ben: And he stole it from somebody else.

Pat: Let's vote whether we keep it or not.

Ben: You'll lose.

Woodstock: I want it.

Ben: Me too. Mother?

Mrs Woodstock: Yes. No. Yes – I don't know. Yes, for Paul's sake.

George: No. It's poison.

June: You're too narrow-gutted ever to own anything. It's yes for me.

Ernest: Next time I set eyes on Thoresby I'll get him. I'm not voting.

Woodstock: Two against, one abstention, and four say yes. We keep it, Ben.

Pat: I knew it was hopeless.

Ben: Why did you get us to vote, then?

Pat: To know where everyone stood.

Mrs Woodstock: She won't throw it in *my* face.

Enter Aslockton.

Pat: Paul will – if ever you see him again.

Woodstock: That's vindictive. Your sorrow's like a bloody overcoat. It keeps you warm, but nobody else.

Woodstock: What do *you* want, Aslockton? Looking for poachers?

Mrs Woodstock: Give him a drink of something.

Ernest: He's had too much already. His throat's gone bang.

Ben hands Aslockton a glass of brandy, but Aslockton looks at it in stupefaction and is unable to drink.

67

Aslockton: Thoresby . . .

Woodstock: Speak up, you bloody vermin. You can't tell *me* anything bad.

Aslockton: Thoresby couldn't.

Mrs Woodstock: Oh, Bernard!

Woodstock: Shut up, everybody.

Aslockton: He shot himself.

Ben: No!

Aslockton: The blinds are drawn.

Ernest: We've been robbed.

Aslockton: He's stone dead.

Ben: No we haven't. Life's cheap around here.

June: (*sobbing*) Paul!

Woodstock: That's bloody fine.

Aslockton: Killed his best dog first. Then blew his face in.

Mrs Woodstock: He did it to spite us.

Woodstock: There's a cold chisel in me.

Ernest: We never did enough for Paul. We didn't look after him.

Mrs Woodstock: Oh, Paul!

Ernest: I'm going for a drive.

Ben: (*fighting to hold Ernest back*) It's no good killing yourself.

Ernest and Ben weep at each other's shoulder.

June: If anybody says a wrong word against our Paul, I'll bloody rend them.

George: What was the point of his life?

Woodstock: I shared his growing pains.

Ernest: (*opening the shooting-stick*) Sit down, father.

Woodstock: To think I liked this field when we came.

Ben: (*to Pat*) I'm sorry.

Pat: There's nothing to say. (*they half embrace, as if to console each other*)

Ben: (*to his mother*) Paul always said: 'Whatever I've got, you can have. I don't want to own anything,' he said. He was younger than me, but he somehow always seemed wiser.

Mrs Woodstock: He was like gold.

Ernest: We should have hanged Thoresby from that tree.

Ben: He beat us to it. The Thoresbys can always go one better than the Woodstocks. We're babies, a pack of bloody know-nothings.

Woodstock: *(standing by the tent door)* I tried, though, didn't I? It's getting light. The clouds are knocking the sun out of shape. It's not even an eclipse. A bloody dish rag flung from somewhere.

Exit Woodstock.

Mrs Woodstock: Let him go.

Ernest: You wouldn't let me go.

George: He won't kill himself.

Ben: He only starts thinking when he's lost something.

Pat: I wonder how he'll explain Paul away now?

Ernest: You want us to be like dumb animals.

Mrs Woodstock: *(to Pat)* He was *our* son, so shut up.

June: Dad doesn't need to explain anything.

Enter Woodstock, limping, his body slightly bent. From now till the end of the act his body becomes more and more twisted.

Woodstock: I'm fed up.

Mrs Woodstock: That's not like you, Bernard.

Woodstock: I know. I've scorned people into stone for saying that. I'm finished.

George: You'll see the rusty side of ninety, dad.

Woodstock: Ben, take over the workshop.

Ben: I don't know anything about machines.

Woodstock: You'll learn.

Ben: Ernest deserves the job more than me.

Ernest: Not if dad says different, I don't.

69

Woodstock: It's an order, not a promotion.

Ben: I can't even use a micrometer.

Woodstock: Learn, then. All that university teaches you to do is bloody-well argue.

Mrs Woodstock: Don't get upset, love.

Woodstock: I'm putting Ben in charge, and that's that. I'm not upset.

Mrs Woodstock: Come on, love, stand up straight.

Woodstock: I can't.

Mrs Woodstock: Let me rub your back. It allus meks you feel better.

June: I'll get the lotion.

Exit June.

Mrs Woodstock: Stand still, love.

Woodstock: Nothing will shift it. It's been at me for days. I didn't feel it though when I was arguing with Thoresby.

Ernest: We'll get one o' them sunray machines, dad.

Woodstock: Take my place in the workshop, Ben, there's a good lad. Paul would have wanted it like that.

Mrs Woodstock: Do as he says.

Ben: Why should I? He's going barmy.

Woodstock: I'm in touch with more than you can imagine in your little mind.

Aslockton: Come on, old pal. We'll pull you through with a bit of a rest. I saw blokes go to pieces in the war. We shielded 'em till they felt all right. Otherwise they'd a run off and the Red Caps would a got them.

Woodstock: (*pushing Aslockton out of the way*) I've lost a son. I'll never know what it's all about. I feel as if I've lived for ever, one life after another blowing me to pieces.

Aslockton: Let's get him to bed. Gi' me a hand, somebody.

Woodstock: It's getting light, but my hands don't move.

70

Mrs Woodstock: Bernie, what is it?

Woodstock: Pins and needles. My legs are clogged. I don't know. I'll be able to see when it gets light again. You know, I don't think I've ever seen properly. Is it getting light yet?

Ernest: Soon, dad.

Woodstock: My eyes are full of blood.

Mrs Woodstock: Let's put you to bed, Bernard.

Woodstock: Don't touch me.

Ernest: Come on, dad.

Woodstock: It's nothing.

Mrs Woodstock: Fill a hot water bottle, there's a good girl.

Pat doesn't move.

Woodstock: I'm frozen in the pod. Unbend me, for God's sake. I can *feel* it getting light. Get the car. We're going to Stafford.

Ernest: Right now?

Woodstock: How do I bloody-well know? Do as I say! I'm not as clapped-out as you all think.

Woodstock collapses.

Aslockton: He's done for.

Enter June with the bottle of lotion.

June: I looked all over the place.

Aslockton: The poor old bugger's having a stroke.

June: Then I found it in the tool kit.

CURTAIN

71

Act Three

SCENE

Interior of the Woodstock workshop in Nottingham three years later. The workshop adjoins the family house.

Down one side is a line of slot-machines. Down the other — a couple of pintable machines, one with its back off.

In the centre is a bench, on which is a slot-machine in process of assembly. Also on the bench is a centre-lathe. To one side is a patched and faded chaise-longue. Tacked on to the wall above is a fly-blown copy of the Factories Act.

Ben, working at the centre-lathe, is wearing a khaki overall-coat, and smoking a cigarette. He wears glasses.

Enter George, pushing an empty trolley. He loads a slot-machine on to it.

Ben: Tested them?
George: They're all right.
Ben: Test 'em.
George: The van's waiting.
Ben: Test the buggers.
George: Keep your shirt on, can't you?

George pulls one handle of a machine, which revolves healthily.

Ben: I wouldn't have one to my back if it was left to you lot. Test 'em.

72

George pulls another handle, and the machine clogs and stops.

Ben: Why does everybody buy our machines and nobody else's? Not because they're cheaper. They break down less, that's why, and it's no bloody thanks to you. Chalk it up to be fixed, and get a reserve from the stores.

Ben returns to his lathe, continues turning the piece of metal. George pulls another machine handle, then another, and both react well.

Enter Ernest.

Ernest: How much longer do I have to wait?

George: I'm testing 'em.

Ernest: I thought you'd done it.

George: It's three times: once when they're finished, once when they're put into the stores, and once when they go out for delivery.

Ernest: You'd think we were making jet engines. Dad thought twice was enough.

Ben: Get a job somewhere else if you don't like it. You're just bone idle and bloody careless, the pair of you.

Ernest: We earn our keep.

Ben: And I treat you like dogs, right? *(telephone rings)* Tell them no.

George: What?

Ben: Just say no. Go on, lift the receiver, open your lips close to the mouthpiece, and make the letters N O – No.

George: *(lifts up the receiver and shouts)* No! *(he pauses, and then puts it down)*

Ben: What did he say?

George: If that's the way you want it.

Ben: He'll buy at my price.

Ernest: We hope so.

Ben: Listen, who jumped the profits up more than double to when dad was alive?

73

George: You did.

Ben: I've got a man in London to oil the business for us as well – a tall, chinless bowler-hatted bastard who has been through Eton, Oxford and the Guards – but by God he knows his stuff.

Ernest: You never get tired of telling us.

Ben: We took over Ron Wiley's business, didn't we? Both of you got off with a fine after that slash-up with the Sproats, but if it hadn't been for that lawyer I found you'd have got eighteen months apiece. Apart from that I've nearly doubled your salaries – and still you complain.

George: We're not happy, that's why.

Ben: Yes, I remember what happiness was like. Two of us died laughing over it.

Ernest: Don't insult dad's memory. Nor Paul's. I'm beginning to hate your guts.

Ben: Old times *are* coming back!

Ernest: We don't even vote any more.

George: *And* we have to clock-in every morning.

Ben: I've made you company directors, haven't I? Looks very posh on your passports.

Ernest: It might, but we're too busy working our guts out to use 'em.

Ben: You've got plenty in the bank, though. What do you think life is? Sitting in a deckchair on Skegness front with bathing beauties going up and down, pouring whisky and soda? Even June's on the board. We might not vote, but we discuss things until everyone is in agreement.

Ernest: Nobody makes a more ruthless businessman than somebody who was once a communist. You were, remember?

Ben: Well, we do drink a bottle of Vodka now and again, don't we? And you can take that as a tribute to the old man's memory. But don't think it's going to go on much longer.

Ernest: Today is July the thirtieth, the day of mourning for dear old Paul, and a tribute to the sacred memory of our father.

Ben: I'll throw mother in as well, if you like.

Ernest: She's not dead yet, you rat. She's still in that nursing home you packed her off to.

Ben: She'll be dead one day. Time doesn't move in mysterious ways. It just kills. Life's cheap. But she's due back today, so stop worrying about that. I'll tell you something else, though: this Day of Death celebration has been going on too long. This is the third and last time we'll do it.

Ernest: We won't stand for it.

Ben: It's just an excuse for a big booze-up in the old style. Even June conceived on the last two occasions of this all too earthy feast.

George: *(picks up a machine-handle)* I'll smash your skull if you don't shut up.

Ben: Save that for the Sproats. They're getting too big for their boots again.

George: Speak fairly, then. We only look forward to the party because there aren't any outings any more.

Enter Aslockton, dressed in his gamekeeper's cap and gaiters. He is stouter now, and has two arms, one of flesh-and-blood as before, and the other such a beautifully made artificial limb that, apart from an occasional stiffness, it looks real. He is pushing a trolley loaded with two slot-machines. He takes them off and sets them down by the bench. Then he crosses round to the front and opens his sandwich packet.

Ernest: Even when we were kids we had plenty. It was marvellous. You might not remember, Ben, because you was only five. The whole gang of us was out in the big car, and we'd had no dinner. Paul was there as well, he was only a baby. Dad stops the car at a shop and buys a pound of Scotch salmon, a tub of Colwick cheese

75

and a box of cakes, and we all set to. He had a wonderful generosity of spirit, dad did!

Ben: I remember. But you can't live on memories.

Ernest: You can make 'em, though.

Enter June, pushing a tea trolley. She wears a blouse and skirt, also has curlers in her hair, and a pair of carpet-slippers on her feet.

George: *(taking out a packet of sandwiches)* Well, you can't deny us a tea break, at least.

Ernest: We've got to watch it, else he would.

Ben: Life wouldn't be worth living if you didn't have to watch it. When you've finished, get those machines delivered. Any trouble from the Sproats, just 'crack a few skulls. Take Wally with you. He's got a good swing of the arm.

Exit Ben.

Ernest: I hate his sarcasm.

George: He was born that way.

June: You want two kids to look after, that'd stop your belly-aching.

June goes around filling their mugs.

Ernest: How does Pat put up with him?

George: She's got to. She's got his kid.

Ernest: We all know whose that was. She married Ben to keep it in the family.

George: The rottener things are the longer they go on.

Ernest: There's worse families than this. Aslockton couldn't stand his, could you, gamekeeper? Left his wife and kids like a shot.

Aslockton: I send 'em plenty of money. They're all at work now, anyway.

George: I expect they were glad to see the back of you.

Ernest: Ben pays him enough. You even got *your* name in the papers after that Sproat clash, Aslockton. Not to mention the best brand new artificial limb that money can buy.

George: More than you ever got from Thoresby.

Ernest: Don't mention that mass-murderer.

Aslockton: It was through you lot he shot himself.

George: Our Paul was worth a hundred of him.

Aslockton: Your Paul was a hooligan who got into a fight he couldn't handle. What else did you expect from Thoresby?

Ernest: Paul was our brother, so shut up.

Aslockton: I lost my job because of him.

George: You got a better one.

Aslockton: I sometimes bloody wonder. *(reaching out and pinching June's arse)* Hello, my love, pour a dose o' that tea into my big gob!

June: George, how much longer are you going to stand for that murderer's murderer handling me?

George: Stop trying to set us at each other's throat.

Ernest: We've had enough bloodshed.

Enter Wally – a stocky man of fifty, all smile and false teeth.

June: Come on and get your tea, Wally.

Ernest: A bit more overtime and you'll be a company director as well.

George: Not to mention a sidesman at chapel.

Aslockton: He lives in the old style, Wally does. Sixty pounds a week, and the pictures on Friday night. A quiet wife and a quiet life. A few prayers on Sunday to keep him at peace with God. What more does a man want?

Ernest: He'll never be happy though till he's seen God on the telly.

June: What's wrong wi' that?

77

Wally stands and straightens the creases in his overalls.

George: Ben knew what he was doing, setting him on. God's own timekeeper: shockproof, waterproof, anti-magnetic and four fake jewels.

Ernest: *(shouts to Wally)* You might be the backbone of society, Wally, but you're turning out *gambling* machines!

June: Leave him alone. You're safe as long as Ben's running things, Wally.

Enter Ben.

June: *(clearing tea mugs away)* What's up now?

Ben: Cancel this morning's plan. Deliver them at six this evening. I've heard the Sproats will be waiting. Phone the arcade and tell 'em, June.

Ernest: Stay where you are. Stop pressing buttons just to watch us jump. You're only trying to get us out of the way so's we shan't be able to have the party. I don't trust you any more.

Ben: You don't? We'll start with you, Wally: do you want your cards?

Wally: *(shakes his head)*

Ben: June?

June: Who'd run the canteen if I was to go?

Ben: George?

George: I've got June and two kids to keep.

Ben: Ernest, that leaves you.

Ernest: You get back to dad's system when it suits you.

Ben: Gamekeeper?

Aslockton: I'm satisfied.

Ben: Get on with the packing, then.

Aslockton: Come on, Wally.

Exit Aslockton and Wally.

78

June: I'll get back to the kids. There's allus somebody to feed.

Exit June, pushing tea trolley.

George: Do we have the party today, or not?
Ben: I don't change plans for nothing.
Ernest: You meant to change them from the start.
Ben: Be reasonable.
Ernest: I always was. That's my trouble.
Ben: Paul wasn't. Look where it got him.
Ernest: And where's all this going to get you?
Ben: I'm doing my duty to you lot, aren't I?
Ernest: We wouldn't starve if you vanished off the face of the earth.
Ben: Nobody starves, these days.
Ernest: It's true, though. You're the strongest in this place.
Ben: Maybe. But it's been an effort for me to get out of the weakness I was born into. I used to think I was a special sort of person, going up through grammar school and getting into university by my own sweat. I used to pity you lot making slot-machines while I sniffed at what it was like to be a student at Cambridge. I suppose I was a communist because I wanted everybody to go there. God! My friends thought father was a factory worker, and I was terrified for the first year in case one of his one-armed bandits found their way there with his little name plate on them. When we met Thoresby it was me who should have been killed, not Paul.
Ernest: Do we have the party, or not?
Ben: We'll have drinks at twelve, then.
George: We'll be there.
Ernest: Come on, let's do the master's bidding.

Exit Ernest and George.

Ben walks to the telephone, and dials.

Ben: Hello? God? This is Ben. Does it matter? Woodstock, then. You know me. I believe in you again. Yes. Did you think about what I said the other day? Why don't you come over – down, then – sometime, when we can have a proper talk. Of course it'd be worthwhile. Yes, I've got a lot to say to you, too. No, I'm not feeling all that good. I don't know why. I've got too many questions. Answer 'em myself? Well, I *am* trying. I feel as though it'll never get dark again. It frightens me. *(shouts):* Bollocks then, if that's how you feel. *(replaces receiver)*

Enter Pat.

Pat: What were you shouting about?
Ben: Keeping my spirits up.
Pat: If that's how you feel, I'm going.
Ben: How's Larry?
Pat: All right.
Ben: Said any new words?
Pat: What do you care?
Ben: I'm always interested in brother Paul's blue-eyed bastard.
Pat: It could just as well be yours.
Ben: Thanks for reassuring me.
Pat: Too much self-pity, that's your trouble.
Ben: It oils the wheels. *(he puts a coin in the machine and pulls the handle)* The fruit of the earth is always on the other side of the glass.
Pat: Why else do you think Bernard Woodstock made such things?
Ben: Oh come on! Why? The slot-machine genius of the age made 'em because that was his version and view of life. Life's a slot-machine: you get out of it what you put into it – except that he got out what other people put in.

He tampered with the mechanism a bit, but it was all the same in the end.

Pat: Your father wasn't as simple as you like to think. All his complexities went into his work. And if ever a man knew his family, he did.

Ben: He knew me. That's why I'm running the firm. But I don't believe in myself because I can't get what I want. And I don't know what I want, so I can't believe in myself. I've got to know that before I can free myself and get anywhere.

Pat: What the Woodstocks want, they get. So I've been led to believe.

Ben: Why do I think I've got nothing, then?

Pat: That's *your* problem.

Ben: We live in the house like lodgers. We don't even sleep together.

Pat: Are you repenting of your charity? Anyway, we voted on it.

Ben: I feel I'm going barmy.

Pat: You're too mean to go mad.

Ben picks up a micrometer at the lathe, and measures the thickness of a steel rod.

Pat: Look, I've spent three years at this place, living in a life-style I'll never get used to even if I stay thirty years. It's a limbo of unresolved conflict and internecine strife. There's no aim, no ambition, no sanity, no peace, and you're the worst bloody boss of a workshop that ever was.

Ben: Everybody's put me on a pedestal here, to save themselves the trouble of thinking.

Pat: *You* let them.

Ben: *(pulls the handle of a machine, and money rolls over the floor)* They pelt me with shit all the time. What else could I do? You get the answers you were born to get.

81

Pat: I suppose you want somebody to hold out a hand and say: 'Come on, Ben, I'll show you the way.'

Ben: *(shouting)* No, I bloody-well don't.

Pat: So, you're coming back to life. We haven't quarrelled so much since that time in Yugoslavia.

Ben: We said we never wanted to see each other again, remember? But five minutes later . . . We're having some drinks at twelve, to remember Paul, and dad.

Pat: Leave me out of it.

Ben: You're part of everything. You're part of me.

Pat: Am I?

Ben: Yes. For ever. Do you remember Greece?

Pat: Sometimes. *(she goes to him)* I wish things could be like that again. It's such a long way off, though, but it haunts me like a dream that seems more real than the life we live now.

Ben: I know what you mean. We've got to get back to it.

Pat: It's no use going back to anything.

They kiss.

Ben: We'll pull it to us, then.

They move to the chaise-longue.

SAME SCENE: LATER.

Stage empty of people. A table with a white cloth spread in the middle of the room.

Enter Aslockton, with a crate on his shoulder, followed by Ernest and June with trays of food.

Aslockton: A dozen bottles of the best. I hope it travels well! *(uncorking a bottle)* In Thoresby's day there was only the gymkhana, and a pint after the tug-o'-war, if we won.

Enter Ben and Pat, carrying a crate of beer between them.

Ernest *(to Aslockton)* You say that every time we have a party – you fraud.

Enter Wally and George.

Pat: Who shall we drink to first?
Ben: Thoresby.
Aslockton: I'll drink to him, any day.
Ernest: *I* bloody won't.
Ben: Woodstock, then, Bernard Woodstock. How's that, Ernest? Our father which art not in heaven and never could be, Bernard Woodstock rotting into worms and coal.
All: Bernard. Woodstock. Father. Dad.

Aslockton fills glasses. George uncorks more wine.

Ben: *Now* Thoresby.
Ernest: Bloody-hell!
Ben: Why not? We can't leave him out – the murdering reactionary who couldn't stand it when someone from a long line of peasants and illiterates went for him.
Ernest: Our Paul wasn't illiterate.

All drink, but in a muted way.

Ernest goes to Ben, and knocks the drink from his glass.

Ernest: You're trying to ruin our celebration.
Ben: *(calmly)* It's only a party, Ernest.

Aslockton refills Ben's glass.

Ernest: Yes, but what would father say?
Ben: He'd shout, till his face was like red cabbage, as he always did.

George: Give me some more, Aslockton.

June: Yes, sweeten everybody up.

Ernest: *(to Ben)* You bastard.

Ben: Have something to eat with it. And don't overdrink, or you'll get too dozy to take those machines out.

Ernest: You're killing everything.

George: Why do we have a party in the middle of the day, then? If it was at night we could go on boozing till we had a blackout.

Ben: It's better this way. Let's drink to the old man again.

Ernest: Dad was a great man.

All: Bernard. Woodstock. Father. Dad.

Ernest: He had a fine life. One of the old sort.

Ben: I know. Poor bloke. As soon as the midwife yanked him out he started to eat his liver. He must have been born with worms, St Vitus's Dance, and the biggest feeling of being persecuted since Machiavelli.

George: Why don't you talk sense?

Ernest: You've got no pity. You'll never understand dad if you've got no pity.

Ben: To mother, then. How's that? She was supposed to be home for the party – but maybe the train was late.

All: To mother!

George: Gis some more booze, Aslockton. Even an angel wouldn't get sloshed on this piss.

Ernest: Aslockton's watered it.

Good-humoured laughter, in which Ben and All join.

Ernest: *(jokingly assuming Woodstock's voice and manner)* It's a shame we didn't get that land, though. You'd have been working for me now, Aslockton.

Ben: He is already – dad!

Aslockton: *(touching his cap)* I am that, Mr Woodstock.

Ben: I'm Lord Thoresby, and it's been in my family for generations.

Aslockton: *(touching his cap again)* It has that, my Lord.

84

Laughter – at this theatrical turn of events.

Ernest: And *you* nicked it from somebody, you land-grabbing old bugger!

Aslockton: And you wanted to nick it back, you know you did. So where's the justice o' that?

All: Boo!

George: It was a lovely field, dad. The air was beautiful. I'll never forget that field.

Aslockton: Before Thoresby shot himself he wanted to come back and pour petrol over your tents.

Ernest: It was *our* land!

Ben: *(Thoresby's voice)*: You pack of Nottingham Bolsheviks!

Laughter.

Aslockton: He could a done. But he was civilised – in the main.

Ernest: No bloody boat to Australia would have been big enough to hold us, Thoresby.

Ben: *(opens a chest and takes out a rifle)* I own that land. If you tread on it, I'll cry.

George: I'm Paul. I'll strangle you. *(to Ernest)*: He's in a wormy state of mind, dad.

Ernest: *(offers Ben a cigar)* No hard feelings, Thoresby. Have a smoke.

Laughter.

Ben: Get off my land. You foul every blade of grass on it.

Ernest: You shot Jack Tibshelf. I suffered like a king in quad.

George: Poor old dad. I'll kill him, dad.

Ben: Get off my land.

George: *(laughing)* What a day *that* was.

Ben: I'll shoot all of you. *(he turns slowly, the gun aimed as if not to lose sight of them)*

Ernest: *(himself again)* Stop it, Ben!

Ben: I'll kill you all.

Ernest: Put that gun down. I'm not dad, I'm your brother.

Ben continues to point the gun. Everyone is afraid, and stare with the same intensity and helplessness as when Thoresby shot Paul.

Ernest: Ben! You're our brother. *(he hits out at him and Ben falls. Lights dim)*

SCENE: SAME. WORKSHOP. LATER.

Ben lies on the sofa. Pat sits by him.

Ben: Where are they?

Pat: Gone to deliver the machines.

Ben: Is my hair the same colour?

Pat: Don't be daft.

Ben: *(sits up)* My face feels like sandpaper.

Pat: You were mad.

Ben: It's all out of us.

Pat: Gone to the middle, you mean.

Ben: If Thoresby had shot himself *after* signing the land over to us, we'd have lost it by some fluke, but at least we could have said we'd owned it, if only for five minutes. It was snatched away from us before our hands could grab it.

Pat: You'll never get over it.

Ben: Why should I?

Pat: I could love you for that.

They kiss.

86

Ben: It's not finished yet. It's hard to get rid of anything in this family. I remember once – I've never told anybody because it was so laughable, I suppose, but I got back late from Cambridge, and only dad was up. He was in a very funny, mellow sort of mood. He went in the kitchen and made some coffee, just for the two of us.

Pat: That's not like bluff Bernard Woodstock.

Ben: I know. He even fried me a couple of eggs at the stove! Then we sat talking for an hour. I was dead on my legs and wanted to sleep, but dad just went on talking. He hardly ever talked to me, but he did that night. He said how proud it made him that I was at Cambridge. As if I didn't know. But I was beginning to despise the place by then. He said he wished *he* could have gone, and had a proper education. He had all sorts of ambitions, and I could hardly believe it when he said he hoped he'd soon have a proper factory – not slot-machines – something that could really expand and become big. He hadn't been drinking. He was ice-sober. He said his biggest ambition was that before he died he'd get a knighthood! I thought his brain was going soft, but he was serious. A knighthood! I pinched myself so that I wouldn't laugh. I even connived at his fantasy, and said maybe it would happen one day. It was hilarious, but I don't laugh any more. Too much has happened. The older I get the less I can laugh at anything. A knighthood! Bernard Woodstock! Can you imagine that?

Pat: Well, yes, I can.

Ben: I used to be frightened of him. We all did. Now I *am* beginning to pity him.

Enter Ernest. He has a gash in his face, and his jacket is over his arm.

Ben pulls the handle of a slot-machine. It doesn't revolve.

Ben: *(laughing)* Chairman of the Chamber of Commerce!

Pat: Member of the Watch Committee!

Ben: Lord Mayor of Nottingham! Sir Bernard Woodstock today opened the new Nottingham Slot-Machine Museum . . .

Ben pulls the handle of a slot-machine forward, and it crashes on to the floor.

Ernest: Do 'em all.

Ben: Something's happened. What is it, then?

Ernest: The Sproats got the kitty. Get me some brandy, Pat.

Ben: What do you mean?

Ernest: What I say.

Ben: Don't drink yourself into a cabbage. I want to know what went wrong.

Enter George – face cut, and clothing torn.

Ernest: They cut us up. The best brandy, Pat – there's nothing like the best when the ruinations are at you. *(to Ben)* The biggest and the best of 'em were waiting for us. *You* couldn't have done any better.

Ernest pours more brandy and swills it over his face, doubling from the pain.

Ben: You fucked it up.

Ernest: You put 'em on to us. You must have done.

Ben: I worked everything out. Someone split.

Enter Wally, bruised and moaning.

Ernest: We drew up to the kerb, suspecting nothing.

Ben: And expecting nothing.

Ernest: Let me finish. The sun was out, so we stamped on our fags and opened the van door. Wally and the gamekeeper rushed to the gate, but it wouldn't open.

George: *He'll* never come back.

Ben: Who?

George: Aslockton. Told the Sproats when and where. It must have been him. Working for them now, you can bet.

Ben: Go on, Ernest.

Ernest: We thought the lock on the gate was jammed, so we started kicking. We expected it to give, but it didn't. Then we humped two machines on the pavement. Didn't we, George? While they were still on our shoulders, though, the Sproat mob ran from round a corner. They'd had time to think about it. I nailed one, George hammered the other. Then the gate opened and four more came out. They smashed the machines, then went for the tyres and headlamps. I slammed a few, but there was too many. Wally got a beating, but Aslockton fell down screaming about his arm. It was a bit funny now I look back on it. Went round to the arcades later, and they don't want our machines any more.

Ben: Where's the van?

George: Still there.

Ben: You lost it.

Ernest: We didn't want to die.

Wally: The other lot were smarter.

Ben: Join them, if you want to.

Wally: I didn't say that.

Ben: June will pay you up.

Wally: Well, I'll never stay where I'm not wanted.

Ben: Get out.

Exit Wally.

George: I used to think he was a fool.

Ben: That made two of you.

Ernest: That leaves you, me and George to run everything.

Ben: Just you and George. Pat and I are leaving.

Ernest: So that's why you just chucked Wally out. You worked for this all along.

Ben: Save yourselves if you want to. We're all equal in the eyes of disaster.

Ernest: Disaster's blind, you damn-fool. We weren't equal when things were all right. Dad would have acted better than this.

Ben: Why do you think he passed everything on to me?

Ernest: To do more than he could do. And you've done it, as well.

Ben: I cut down the number of creditors: there'll be a good bit of money to share out.

Enter Mrs Woodstock, wearing hat and fur coat.

Ernest: You're our brother. We put all our faith in you, and as soon as something goes wrong you want to bale out. Hello, ma! All for that false wife Paul shoved on to you, and that kid that was never yours. *She* put you up to this.

Pat: You're a liar, as well as a fool.

Ben: Don't worry, love. It's me they want. This is the house of human sacrifice.

Pat: I'm going to feed Larry.

Exit Pat.

Ben: You never got out of the blood-age. How was I born into such a family? I don't fit, and never did.

Mrs Woodstock: You're my son, anyway. And Bernard's. A real chip off the old block. Bernard often wanted to pack things in, but I talked him out of it – as he wanted me to. I was the one as kept him going.

Ernest: Hello, ma! We make a good living, don't we? And now you want to give it up. Nobody slaves for a boss if they can make a living on their own.

Ben: (*kisses his mother*) Glad to see you back. Dad always

90

used to talk about his 'trade', as if he were a skilled mechanic, but he was a plain racketeer, worse than old Thoresby who was just a medieval plunderer in modern dress. They got on well at the end, I remember, the two of them. Dad always wanted to be normal, and respected, though, but he knew it was useless, and that if ever he tried to raise above what he was born to be he'd get kicked down again. Blokes like him, and like us, aren't liked in this country. He was ingenious, all the same, with machinery.

Ernest: Everything will fall apart if you go, Ben.

Mrs Woodstock: No it won't *(she takes off her hat and coat)* I'm glad to be back, though I appreciated that few months of peace at the Home. I was sorry I got back too late for the celebrations for father and Paul. Where's June?

Ernest: Cooking the books, I suppose.

George: She's feeding something or other.

Mrs Woodstock: I do like everyone to be here when I come home.

George: I'll tell her.

Exit George.

Mrs Woodstock: The matron gave me a little party last night because I was leaving. Champagne and chicken. I was cheerful all the way down. Which is more than I can say for you two. Come on, crack the ice and say hello!

Ben: Welcome back, mother.

Mrs Woodstock: Thank you, dear.

Ernest: Hello, ma!

Mrs Woodstock: Let's see you smile then, Ben.

Enter George and June.

Mrs Woodstock: Come on, George, I ought to get a kiss from my son-in-law at least. Let me wash that blood off your face, Ernest. I do wish you wouldn't fight. It don't become grown men. It breaks my heart when you won't tell me your troubles, Ben.

Ben: I can't.

Mrs Woodstock: You always did know how to make me happy.

Ernest: Well *he* sent you away, ma, and that was a fact. We came back from a job one day, and you'd gone. As quick as that. Then he talked about how it was best for everybody's good till we couldn't stand it any longer. As if he wanted you out of the way while he did summat wicked.

Mrs Woodstock: You and George let him do it, don't forget. Don't think I relished being pushed off.

Ernest: When Ben gets anything into his moody loaf nobody can do a thing about it.

Mrs Woodstock: Don't think I like coming back all that much either. I was near to getting married again. One of the gardeners thought enough of me to ask, but I was more concerned about you lot.

June: You should have done, ma. It'd have served 'em right.

Mrs Woodstock: What a welcome! My favourite son about to leave home, and Bernard's business going down. Wally spilled the news as I came in. Tears in his eyes, as he opened the door of my taxi.

Ben: I gave him his cards. He was no good.

Mrs Woodstock: I knew something was up. There always is. I'd like us to go to that field in Staffordshire, Ben, a little act of remembrance for Paul and Bernard, where we can hold hands for a moment and let bygones be bygones. We might prosper after that.

Ben: I hate the place.

Ernest: Don't you respect anybody's wishes?

Ben: When I went to London a month ago, I had a look at that field on the way back. I found it all right – on my old one-inch map. But I thought I was on the moon.

The lane was a muddy dual carriageway of lorries and mechanical diggers, and the field had had its top ripped off. The pretty wood had gone, and tons of opencast coal were being pulled out of its guts.

Enter Pat.

Ben: Larry all right?
Ernest: Don't cry, ma. He's as twisty as Old Nick's bootlace.
Pat: Eating like a trooper.
George: What was the point of telling her that?
Ernest: I'll never forgive you.
Ben: You'd be spineless enough to lie. We can manage without our little patch of sacred earth.
Mrs Woodstock: Get those fists down, Ernest. Haven't you had enough for one day?
Ben: Let him come.
Mrs Woodstock: Now stop it, both of you. I bought a cake from that patisserie outside the station. We can eat it for our tea. You won't go, will you, Ben?
Ernest: He'll run like a shot rabbit. Think of dad: hard times was the breath of life to him. If he got in this fix he'd a bin round at the Sproats already, sorting things out. There'd have been blood and money flying everywhere.
Mrs Woodstock: Only after I prodded him he would.
Ben: Yes, he died of a stroke at sixty.
Ernest: You think it's fun to smash things down. But you're just losing your grip. You've gone weak all of a sudden.
Ben: I could sort the Sproats out in ten minutes if I wanted. But my weakness was having a father like Bernard Woodstock. Because no toffee-nosed self-respecting member of society would have anything to do with him he had to torment and dominate his family as if they were a rival gang trying to do him out of his

business. In his spot-on cunning he saw that I was the only one who'd be able to do things in the way *he'd* always wanted to do them. And I've been fool enough to accept it as a flattering testimony to my own vain merits. Oh, he knew my weakness all right.

Mrs Woodstock: You're an ungrateful son, talking about my husband like that.

Ben: That's how I feel, mother. I'm sorry.

Mrs Woodstock: He knew your strength as well. I will say that for him. He did allus want people to think better of him. You're right there.

Ben: His shabby little slot-machine industry is finished from this moment on. He had his last fling when he tried to get hold of Thoresby's land. He knew he was going to die right enough, but he was never one to spare the feelings of those he was leaving behind.

Ernest: There's no point in hating the old man.

Ben: I don't give him that much power. The only time I thought history was on his side was when he tried to get land from Thoresby. I'm no longer part of that. All history is theft.

Mrs Woodstock: You do hate him, though. And that's no good, Ben. Is it, George?

Ernest: Running away is suicide.

Ben: It's self-preservation.

June: The trouble with running away is that sooner or later you run into what you're running away from – like Bernard did.

Ben: Uh?

George: Good old June!

Ernest: If you go, you'll leave all your troubles with us. Generosity itself. That's you, Ben. Thanks.

Pause of silence from All.

Ben: I've got *something* to say.

Ernest: Here comes the Riot Act.

George: Let's hear it.

Ben: We don't make any more slot-machines or one-armed bandits – or pintable machines or gambling rigs of any kind – any more.

Ernest: What are we going to make, then? Locomotives, radiograms, Bailey bridges? We're all jigged up for slot-machines. We can make 'em blindfold – and sell all we make. We even exported some to Holland last year.

Ben: We'll phase out gradually and bring in new products.

Ernest: It's senseless. We could never do it.

Ben: *(shouts)* You greedy bastards. You'd rip my heart out if you could. I want to do it for all of us.

Pat: Sounds as if you're in love again. I was beginning to worry.

Mrs Woodstock: All men are brothers, as your dad used to say.

Ben: I don't give a damn if people think we're a lot of racketeers and upstarts. That's nothing to do with us. It's their problem. That's why they kill each other. We'll make anything though, but not slot-machines. And we want more people in the firm. The family needs thinning out a bit.

Ernest: What's wrong with slot-machines? People love 'em, don't they? Have you been in Smithy's arcade on Saturday night and seen 'em shoving their shillings in? They've got ecstasy on their faces, Ben, ecstasy.

Ben: Yes, the ecstasy of death. We'll make other things.

Ernest: It won't work.

Ben: The workshop's full of machinery. I'll plan the take-over. There's enough money in the bank to buy that place next door *and* get more machines. It'll be WOODSTOCK BROTHERS: GENERAL ENGINEERING. You remember that 'Simplified Typewriter For A Child Of Six That Will Last A Lifetime' I was telling you about? That's one of the things we can make. We'll call it The Chimp – Woodstock's Chimp. Oh yes, we'll bang up the export trade – one of England's labour intensive workshops, succoured by pride, ingenuity, and high quality. We'll even export things to Hong Kong. That'll get us a write-up in the *Sunday Times*!

Pat: I'm with you, Ben.

Mrs Woodstock: You can give me a job in the firm, too.

Ernest: We'll hold him to that.

Ben embraces Pat.

Ben: You won't regret it?

Pat: I love you.

Ben: You won't regret that, either.

Pat: I will, a thousand times. I only say I love you because I know I'll regret it. You don't want a happy ending, do you? I always thought you harboured a death-wish.

Ben: It's been chopped out of me.

Pat: Good. Otherwise I'd leave you.

Ben: You want everything.

Pat: Don't *you*?

Ben: Yes. And I'll get it.

Pat: So will I.

Ernest: It frightens me to death.

George: I'm willing to make the change.

Mrs Woodstock: Good lad, George.

June: It's all right by me.

Pat: Ernest?

Ernest: Nobody's going to draw the curtain on this family. I mean firm.

Ben: It takes a long time to get round to where you wanted to be in the first place.

Ernest: Running away's no good. I know that much.

Ben: *(takes tea and piece of cake)* Thanks, ma.

Ernest: Ta, ma.

Ben: The only thing left is survival, and that means knowing what you want.

Ernest: You've got Pat, anyway.

Pat: You mean I've got him.

Ernest: What the Woodstocks want, they get.

George: Once they know what they want.

Pat: If a man won't tell you what he wants it means he wants something so much that nothing will stop him getting it. Right, Ben?

Ben: Right. I know what I want now.

Ernest: That means we've really got to keep our eyes on each other.

Ben: We have. But I'm not asking for your opinion.

Ernest: Well, you're getting it, and you'll get plenty more from now on.

Ben: We'll sort out those blueprints in the morning. That's when I'll be asking for opinions.

Mrs Woodstock: *(softly but firmly)* Stop it, all of you. Let's think of Bernard and Paul for a moment. Then we can get back to work.

SILENCE

CURTAIN

THE INTERVIEW

A one-act play

People

Soviet Officer
Prisoner of Conscience
Irina Krichev

THE INTERVIEW

SCENE

Somewhere in Moscow. A Soviet Officer is standing pensively by a chair in the middle of a large room. There is a prominent and framed picture of Lenin on one wall. A few feet away is a desk. The telephone on it begins to ring. He walks over to answer it.

Officer: Yes, Comrade-General, I'm waiting for them now. Born, sir? Where was *I* born? It's all in the records, Comrade-General. I was born in Kromy, Orel Province. April 27th, 1922. That's where I first saw light, sir, as one of our novelists might say! Yes, sir, my mother wiped my nose quite often. Naturally. So did my father. *(laughs: uneasily)* He threw me up in the air, and always caught me – providing he was drunk! Orel, sir, 1922. Thank you, sir.

Officer puts down the telephone with a laugh – as if he is being watched, or listened to.

Officer: Bloody sense of humour. Good sense of humour!

Officer walks up and down his office. He pauses by the chair. He straightens the creases in his trousers. While talking (in the following monologue) he adjusts his tie, smooths his hair, puts his hat on and takes it off.

Officer: What the devil did he want to know that for? Of course my mother wiped my nose. Quite often, as a matter of fact. Who else would do it? It's a perfectly normal thing. He only dropped me twice. From then on my mother made sure he didn't get near me. Not when he'd had a few, anyway. I loved him, though. He was my best friend – till I went to school and joined the Young Pioneers. Then I moved to the High School, and on to University. Why not? I didn't graduate. I joined the Party, and during the Great Patriotic War I kept the supply columns moving to Warsaw and Berlin. And back again, naturally. Well, somebody had to pay for all we'd lost.

The telephone rings. He answers it, believing it to be the General again, whereas it is some lesser person.

Officer: Orel, sir, 1922. Oh no, nothing. Yes, all right. I'll just let them talk. No, I won't. I'll listen, just as you say. Let *him* come in first.

Enter Prisoner of Conscience – a man of about forty, in plain clothes. He walks slowly, obviously tired.

Officer walks to him in the middle of the room, and offers a cigarette. He passes it over singly from the packet, and then a box of matches with a match on top of the box.

Prisoner lights his own cigarette with the single match – staring at the flame till it reaches his fingers. Then he blows it out, and passes the matchbox back.

Officer: Did they feed you?
Prisoner: *(nods)*
Officer: Then you've got nothing to complain about.
Prisoner: I never complain.
Officer: Wouldn't do you much good.
Prisoner: It's a long way from Mordovia. That's an observation, not a complaint.
Officer: They put you on the 12.32 yesterday from

Syzran, and you got here this morning. Quick. They'll be moving you about by plane next.

Prisoner: Stinking planes, if they do. They drove me to Penza, and the train stopped specially for *us* to get on. What's it all for?

Officer: They didn't tell you?

Prisoner: I'm to be a witness. And good luck to you, they said. A trip to Moscow thrown in. Last night they even brought me a meal from the dining car. I couldn't believe it.

Officer: I hope you enjoyed it.

Prisoner: I threw up afterwards.

Officer: Bad digestion. Pity.

Prisoner: There aren't enough medicines in camp. Not for us, anyway.

Officer: You weren't brought here to tell me that.

Prisoner: True. It's just another observation. They even gave me breakfast this morning. I enjoyed that. I kept it down.

Officer: You do get *some* medicines in camp, though.

Prisoner: What do you mean?

Officer: I mean – extra medicines. Pills, penicillin. That sort of thing. Oh, don't worry. We know all about it. It comes in quite openly – by post sometimes. Or visitors bring it.

Prisoner: Oh, so that's it.

Officer: We know who's behind it. But a few medicines or a bit of food – there's nothing wrong with that.

Prisoner: We get what's left after the guards have rummaged through it.

Officer: That's more than you deserve. But you also get radio parts, and books, propaganda. That's more serious. The guards don't get an opportunity to rummage through that.

Prisoner: I don't know anything about it.

Officer: We didn't expect you to. We're realistic. I've worked in the camps. But I've got your file here. It says you were a radio engineer, from Berdichev. I never did like Berdichev. It's a deadbeat miserable place. Went through it by train once, and didn't even get off.

Prisoner: 'Balzac was married in Berdichev.'

Officer: Hey? Who?

Prisoner: Balzac – he was happy in Berdichev.

Officer: *(writing)* Bal-zac. Balzac. Funny name.

Prisoner: He was a novelist. French. *I* was happy there, as well.

Officer: You might be happy there again if you do as you're told. What do you say?

Prisoner: Five years ago I asked for a visa to go to Israel. But instead I got eight years for embezzling.

Officer: *(looks)*

Prisoner: Among other things.

Officer: What's done is done. Why harp on that? You had a fair trial, and were found guilty. All open, with witnesses.

Prisoner: Witnesses were easy to find. You threaten someone. Or you promise something. A witness is only a man or woman, after all. One of them was even supposed to be my friend.

Officer: Lies. You're only saying that because you think you've nothing to lose. *Everyone* has something to lose.

Officer takes a cigarette from his pocket, and offers it in the same style as last time.

Prisoner takes it, and puts it into his jacket pocket.

Officer: Why are you saving it? There are plenty more.

Prisoner: If I smoke another so soon, I'll be ill.

Officer: You've a lot to gain, a man in your position. You could be out and free if you co-operate with us today. We might even let you go to America. You'll enjoy the race-riots, and unemployment, and the gangsters everywhere!

Prisoner: I don't want to go to America.

Officer: England, then. The fog and the dirt should suit you. You'll wear a straw hat and carry a walking stick to poke beggars out of the way. You'll never find a place as good as the Soviet Union.

Prisoner: I don't want to go to England, either.

Officer: Good old Mother Russia looks after her own. But we know where the likes of you want to go, don't we?

Prisoner: I've never made a secret of it.

Officer: All right, then. Wherever you like. Maybe even Israel, if you tell us who brings in the spare radio parts, and the books, and all the Zionist propaganda.

Prisoner: I'll tell you the truth.

Officer: Good!

Prisoner: You won't like it.

Officer: The truth is all I want.

Prisoner: I know. But whose truth?

Officer: There's only one truth. On my name-day my father once gave me a History of the Communist Party of the Soviet Union. It told me how we built this great society of ours, with the whole world at our throat like a pack of wolves. It cost us millions of good people to get where we are today, and now anti-soviet worms like you want to smash it all down.

Prisoner: *My* truth is different. I'll tell you . . .

Officer: Shut up! The truth is what *we* say, and what we tell *you* to say. Don't you dare forget it, or you'll go back to Mordovia on your hands and knees. You'll eat mud – every millimetre of the way, if we let you. That's the truth, you bone-idle parasite!

Prisoner: I've eaten mud already – and worse.

Officer: Worse? There's no such thing as worse than what we can do to you.

Prisoner: I'll tell you the truth. But I'm sure you won't like it. The truth is – that nobody brings radio parts, or books, into the camp.

Officer: That's what I thought you would say. You're

a clever man. A real Jew! Now, you want *me* to tell *you* who brings them in! You want suggestions. You don't want the responsibility of even thinking up the names of the people you're going to testify against. All right: but watch yourself. Don't forget that if you let me down I can be a bastard as well. We didn't bring you all this way for a trip through the country-side, and a picnic at the end of it. You aren't here to pick mushrooms.

Prisoner: I didn't think I was. Too many mushrooms are poisonous.

Officer: Yes, you're an intelligent man. You'd be no good to us if you weren't.

The telephone rings.

Officer: *(into the 'phone)* Give me a few more minutes. Let her wait.

Prisoner: You didn't bring me here to flatter me, either. I can see that.

Officer: I'm going to tell you who is responsible for bringing all those things into the camp. And you're going to prove it – by denouncing her.

Prisoner: You want me as a witness.

Officer: She's been coming here shouting for a visa for years, and she's coming again this morning. We must put a stop to it. If we succeed maybe others will give up as well, and we can lead useful lives again.

Prisoner: I suppose I'm allowed to ask who she is.

Officer: Well, it is a witness's privilege. Her name's Krichev – Irina Krichev.

Prisoner: I seem to remember the name.

Officer: That should make it easier.

Prisoner: But I forget where I heard it.

Officer: Think.

Prisoner: She's Jewish.

Officer: Why else should she want to go to Israel.

Prisoner: So am I.

Officer: *(laughs)* We choose our witnesses carefully. They have to be convincing. We don't want any old anti-social ragbag who'd jump at the chance to testify against his own mother for a crust of bread! Plenty of those around. Oh no – we want a man of principle, an intelligent fellow like yourself.

Prisoner: I might not agree to it.

Officer: You want to go free, don't you?

Prisoner: Yes.

Officer: You want to be able to go back to Berdichev, to your family, to walk the streets, meet friends, eat all you like?

Prisoner: I do.

Officer: Bump into this Balzac friend you mentioned?

Prisoner: Of course.

Officer: Isn't that worth a lot to you? Everything? Do as I say. Just listen. You'll soon see how easy it will be to denounce her. She'll incriminate herself.

Prisoner: How can you be so sure?

Officer: They all do. She wants a visa to go to Israel!

Prisoner: So do I.

Officer: Denounce her, then!

Before the Prisoner can answer, the Officer picks up the telephone.

Officer: You can send her in now.

Prisoner takes his cigarette out, and lights it.

Enter Irina Krichev, a woman in her forties.

Officer: Come in.

Irina: Oh.

Officer: Don't mind him.

Irina: All I want is . . .

Officer: We'll find out what you want in due course. But you're lucky, you know. I'll tell you that for a start.

Irina: Who is he?

Officer: Nobody. Sit down.

Irina: *(remains standing)*

Officer: You're lucky to be talking to me in a nice free-and-easy way.

Irina: But *you* are talking to me.

Officer: All right: why did you come here today?

Irina: You know why. I didn't want to.

Officer: Sit down. We've got better things to do than waste time on you.

Irina: You force me to come here. I queue for a bus. I get crushed on the underground. I walk through the snow. And when I get here I walk along all those endless corridors with people waiting in them. I felt faint and ill, and thought I would fall. A young man took my arm. He helped me. You do sometimes find good people in unexpected places. Then I'm told to wait – and wait. You think I like coming here?

Prisoner: All we can do is talk. Otherwise the heart bursts.

Officer: I'll tell you when *you* can talk. *And* what to say.

Irina: I've been here so many times before. I've forgotten how often.

Officer: Well, why *do* you come, then? You only waste your time. Not to mention mine.

Irina: Let me go.

Officer: Go on, then. Nobody's stopping you. Our streets are clean enough for you to walk on, aren't they?

Irina: I want to go to Israel. To my own country.

Officer: You're in your own country.

Irina: I'm a Jew.

Officer: You're a Soviet citizen.

Irina: It says 'Jew' on my passport, so my country is Israel.

Officer: Yes, I know: as soon as you get a visa you run off to America. We know you lot.

Irina: I want to go to Israel.

Officer: Well, all right. Israel. We're reasonable. We're democratic. Socialist legality is for everyone – even you, finally. But there are some forms to fill in.

Irina: I've done all that before.

Officer: It makes no difference.

Irina: I can do it blindfold.

Officer: I'll do it for you this time. What's your name?

Irina: Irina Krichev.

Officer: Good. What year were you born?

Irina: You're not writing.

Officer: I am. What year did you say?

Irina: 5692.

Officer: *(starting to write)* 569 . . . What the hell does that mean?

Irina: The year of my birth.

Prisoner: According to the Jewish Calendar.

Irina: 5692.

Officer: There's only one calendar in the Soviet Union. The 'Old Style' went out before the Revolution. How old are you?

Irina: As old as anti-semitism.

Officer: That's an old one! You've been listening·to foreign radio stations, maybe. Or perhaps they've been listening to your lies. *(to prisoner)* Can a home-made transmitter be heard in the West?

Prisoner: Yes.

Officer: From the camps, I mean?

Prisoner: If I made one, it could. But I never made one. How can I make valves and condensers – or transmitters – out of bread and old copies of *Pravda*?

Officer: I want a serious answer.

Prisoner: Yes – then.

Officer: Yes – what?

Prisoner: Yes – plain and simple.

Officer: We'll come back to that. *(to Irina)* Anti-semitism doesn't exist in our socialist country.

Irina: It does. They call it anti-Zionism now – just another brand of anti-semitism. Every Jew feels it, whether they want to go to Israel or not.

Officer: That is slander, comrade.

Irina: Anti-Zionism is anti-semitism. Show me that it isn't. Prove it doesn't exist.

Officer: Our Constitution says so – in so many words.

Irina: I'll believe it when those of us who applied to go to Israel have been given our jobs back. And then I'll believe it again when all of us who want visas have been allowed to leave.

Officer: That's what we're here to talk about. Your husband was given permission. He was lucky. So was your sister.

Irina: That was a year ago. Now I want to join them.

Officer: We'll have to see about that. Age?

Irina: Forty-five.

Officer: Where were you born?

Irina: Born?

Officer: Yes, born. Where were you born?

Irina: I haven't been born – yet.

Officer: I don't understand. Do you want to live? If you do, don't talk in riddles. Just answer a few simple straightforward questions.

Irina: When a vital question of life and death keeps getting 'NO' for an answer nothing is straightforward any more. If I thought so I'd go insane. I'm not like you. Life is simple, and good – for you. You're in your own country, so you were born when you were born. Just like that. But I'm not in my own country – yet. I'll be born when I'm in Israel, when I can walk in the streets of Jerusalem. They sent me pictures, so I know what it looks like. I'll touch its walls and stones with these hands. *Then* I'll be born. I'll be able to breathe, then.

Officer: That's all very well. But you're forty-five years of age, so you must already have been born somewhere.

Irina: Perhaps.

Officer: *(shouts)* You're breathing, aren't you? *(pause) Aren't* you? *(as if there might be some doubt)*

Irina: I was born . . . in Novorossisk.

Officer: That's more like it. When?

Irina: Last year.

Officer: *(exasperated)* What the devil does that mean?

Irina: I was born last year, so that I could say: 'Next year in Jerusalem!'

Officer: Jerusalem! What the hell *is* this Jerusalem?

Irina: The capital of Israel. In Zion.

Prisoner: Russian Christians used to *walk* there – from Moscow – even Siberia.

Irina: I'd walk there, if they'd let me.

Officer: In those days they didn't know any bettter. They were starving, out of work, illiterate, ignorant, dirty and superstitious. We've altered all that. Now people have shoes on their feet, and coats on their backs. That's what Marxism-Leninism has done. They don't want to run away to some filthy place and worship a god who only wants to keep 'em miserable. Anyway, you were born in Novorossisk.

Irina: Yes. It's on the Black Sea.

Officer: *(writing)* Novo-rossisk. I was there once for three months. Marvellous, easy-going people down there. It's a fine town. Worth ten Jerusalems. A beautiful part of the Great Soviet Motherland. 'A garden watered with champagne', as one of our poets said.

Prisoner: There's a bitter north-east wind, though, all the same. I was there, too.

Officer: Maybe there is, but it isn't grabbed from someone else, like the place you Jews want to go to.

Irina: Novorossisk only belonged to Russia since 1829. You grabbed it from the Turks and the Caucasians.

Officer: That's Zionist propaganda, obviously.

Irina: It's history.

Officer: It's bloody traitors' history.

Irina: My father was a loyal Bolshevik. He was a member of the Communist Party, and knew Stalin – for his sins. He was killed with the Red Army fighting at Stalingrad, when I was eleven. My mother died in 1963.

Officer: You're right. That was a loyal generation. They worked and they fought, and they didn't come troubling us for visas to go to Israel. They got what-for in those days.

Prisoner: They still do.

Officer: They got shot for a stray word. They got twenty-five years for a look we didn't like. They got ten to remind the others to get on with their work. They were loyal, right enough.

Irina: I remember. But these days aren't exactly good for *us*, either.

Officer: They'll get worse if you don't get back to a normal life and stop pestering us.

Irina: How can I? My life here is finished. There's nothing normal any more. If I don't get a visa I'll keep coming back.

Officer: You'll be wasting our time. Why don't you learn?

Irina: And I'll come back again.

Officer: We have more to do than bother with people like you.

Irina: And I'll come back again.

Officer: We want to build communism instead of wasting time with all this.

Irina: Communism without freedom is not worth building.

Officer: Isn't it? The people have work now, and food, and shelter. They have radio sets and television. *That's* freedom. Go on to the street and ask whether they'd rather have all that – or the sort of freedom *you* want. They'll make short work of you.

Irina: I only want to be free to go. It's six years since I

112

first came to ask for a visa. I was thrown out of my job for it. They didn't give me any reason, but they knew they didn't need to.

Officer: *(reading from papers)* We refused you a visa because your work as a costing accountant at the Moscow Institute of Hydrology and Microbiological Synthesis for Planning and Production put you in contact with state secrets. A perfectly good reason. We're not so untidy!

Irina: Do you know what those secrets were?

Officer: I don't want to know.

Irina: I reported on the standards of hygiene in foodshops. What's secret about that? It's nothing to do with tanks or planes.

Officer: Or radio sets concealed in food? In tins and bottles of food?

Irina: I don't know what you mean, but I found out where rats and mice build their nests, what sort of cheese they liked, and how they could open tins of meat with their sharp little teeth – not to mention what blackmarket fiddles were going on in some places. But I lost that job because I wanted to go to Israel. And they sent me to work in a geriatric hospital as a sort of punishment. But I did it. *(she holds up her hands)* Why not? We're all workers, aren't we?

Officer: That sort of work is a luxury. *I* could tell you about *work* if I wanted to. Real work. I've seen them working in the forests near Magadan in winter. I've seen them labouring at Vorkuta.

Prisoner: Have *you* laboured at Vorkuta yourself, though? Sweated in rags at Karaganda? I know you haven't. Work glorified by those who don't dirty their hands is worse than slavery for those who have to. I've heard it all before, but in this office it sounds even more obscene than when it's barked at us in the wilderness.

Officer: You speak when I want you to, or else . . .

Prisoner: You brought me here for a purpose. You want

me to bear false witness. All right. But you don't have to insult me as well. I didn't come here to . . .

Officer walks across to Prisoner – and looks into his face, as if he will knock him down. But he controls himself – or decides not to – and says with menacing calm:

Officer: Sing when I tell you to, and not before, jailbird. If you must talk, talk about the radio sets you build from pieces which she and her friends smuggle into camp. We're civilised now. We don't work people to death any more. Do we? *Do* we?

Prisoner: No.

Officer: That's better. There are still too many idlers, though. But we'll deal with them, don't worry.

Irina: I still work. I've got a job as a nanny now, looking after a little boy. I love him very much. And he loves me. *(she sits down at last)* I only ask you to give me a visa.

Officer: *(briskly, now that he seems to have cowed them both)* That's more like it. Now there's one more question to ask. It's not on the visa form.

Prisoner: Most questions aren't. When I wanted a visa, I ended up in a prison camp.

Officer: Shut up.

Prisoner: I said something I wasn't supposed to say.

Officer: You'll get twenty-five years.

Prisoner: My only luxury is talk.

Officer: Talk in the right way, then. You play ball with us, and we'll play ball with you. Understand?

Prisoner: Yes.

Officer: Now you've got no excuse.

Irina: Who are you?

Prisoner: I'm worse off than you. And better off, at the same time.

Irina: You're a prisoner? I thought you were an engineer.

Prisoner: I was – radio. In the prison camp I built a vast broadcasting station under one of the huts, a 500-kilowatt transmitter, with scores of studios for putting out new broadcasts and staging plays. There was a 100-metre aerial-mast on top with a flashing light to warn low-flying aircraft that they were in danger of colliding with Radio Mordovia's clandestine broadcasting station. All of it was built out of food-scraps and rags, discarded bottles and tins, and old motor-tyres that you and all my Zionist friends sent into the camp by registered letter and undiscovered tunnels!

Officer: A psychiatric hospital is what you need. Yes, a bit of the old needle to set you straight again. Maybe for both of you.

Prisoner: The most a few Jewish prisoners could manage in our strict regime camp was to get enough candles to light for Hanukkah the night before I left. Someone had made a menorah out of wood and put the candles in, and lit them from left to right when a watcher at the door saw the first three stars in the sky. The candles had to burn then for at least half an hour, and after the *ma'ariv* we were anxious in case they didn't. No one dared to disturb the service. Before prison camp I'd never even seen a Hanukkah candle because my family wasn't religious. That was the only transmitter I saw – the flame of a candle.

Officer: You can't mystify me with all that mumbo-jumbo. Prisoners of every sort turn religious in their bigoted reactionary way.

Prisoner: They suffer. When man fails, they turn to God. We were only there because we were Jews.

Officer: You're convicted criminals, and deserve all you get.

Irina: I was asked to come here to see about my visa.

Officer: That's right. And when you've told us all we want to know you can go home, and have a long rest till we need you again. If you don't stay away you may be charged with smuggling radio parts into the camps. We already have witnesses lined up.

Irina: I expect you have. You put us beyond the law.

Officer: We don't want to. You do it yourselves. All you have to do is tell me who the others are. There *are* more. We *know*. *(Officer passes Irina a sheet of paper)* Write down their names.

Irina: There are names already written on it.

Officer: Do you know them?

Irina: No.

Officer: Come on, who do you know?

Irina: Nobody.

Officer: Sign it.

Irina: *(hands the paper back to the Officer)*

Officer: Agree to give up this stupid visa business.

Irina: At the demonstration in memory of our people who were murdered by the Germans (and their willing helpers) at Babi Yar, I was arrested and beaten up.

Officer: We don't like demonstrators – or demonstrations of any sort. Only tidy official ones.

Irina: When Israel took part in the World Student Games I was knocked about by young Soviet soldiers.

Officer: You were making trouble. Our citizens live orderly lives. They behave themselves. Just sign a paper saying you'll never ask for a visa again.

Irina: All we ask for is the legal and human right to cross frontiers. It's a basic need – a human right.

Officer: Human rights! That's all I hear. You want your human rights at other people's expense. Your sort would crawl over anybody to get your own way. You've done no more than anybody else to deserve human rights.

Prisoner: Yes, she has. I know you now. We've talked about you. She's the person who sends letters and parcels to Jewish prisoners – vitamins, food, medicines – things that encourage us to go on living. She keeps us from despair, a risky and perilous thing for her to do, it seems.

Officer: Now you're saying the right things. Tell us how she and her Zionist network get Hebrew papers, books, radio sets inside to you. Well, come on. I want to hear it.

Irina: It's a lie.

Officer: We have proof. We've got twenty witnesses. Our friend here is ready to testify.

Irina: It's all lies.

Officer: So you won't admit anything? It'll do you no good. We'll get you, your family, your friends. We'll round up the whole lot of you.

Irina: I have nothing to say.

Officer: We've got a witness – but it'll be better for you if *you* tell us everything first.

Irina: I know nothing.

Officer: Our country is big, a great nation. It's magnanimous and just. We've made mistakes, I know. But there's a place in it for everybody. You've been educated here. We need your talent, your skills and good-will to help us build a society for the people. If you say no more about a visa for Israel, things could go much better for you.

Irina: Oh, I don't judge this country. I wish all of you well. But I don't belong here, nor do other Jews who want to leave.

Officer: We don't give up our people so easily.

Prisoner: If you gave all of us visas, the necessary paper would use up only one small Russian tree. There are millions beyond the camp wire.

Officer: I don't understand you. I frankly don't. You were born here. We feed you, educate you, protect you, and then you up and say: Thank you very much, but now I want to go to Israel. Is that fair?

Prisoner: It costs us nine hundred roubles to get that pink slip of paper called a visa.

Officer: That nine hundred roubles pays for *nothing*. You've had the best education we could give you, something beyond price. We stinted nothing at a time when the country was often unable to afford even the basic necessities for other people. Don't whine to me about the nine hundred roubles.

Irina: We Jews have given so much for Russia. We've worked for it, and been worked to death for it. You can never repay us for all we've done. The marks of our loyalty will be here for decades. But some of us have had enough. I want to go to my own country where I won't be followed in the street, where I can be telephoned without hindrance, where I can get telegrams and letters freely. If I go to Israel you won't need to have a car full of able-bodied men following me everywhere. They're stronger than I am. They eat more. You pay them more – I'm certain of that. *They* can carry bricks and mix mortar. Let them build communism in my place.

Officer: They're working already, vital work against the enemies of our society. If it weren't for you and your friends they certainly would be doing better things.

Prisoner: If *she* goes, she'll be missed by a lot of people.

Officer: She won't go. *(to Irina):* Don't think your words will be forgotten.

Irina: I suppose all I say here *is* being recorded. Even when I'm in my own room, I expect it is.

Officer: We've got places for people like you.

Irina: If you put me away someone else will step into my shoes – till everybody who wants to go has gone.

Telephone rings. Officer lifts the receiver, and answers:

Officer: No Comrade-General. Not yet, sir. Thank you, sir. *(replaces the receiver)*

Irina: The more I ask for a visa, the more I suffer for it.

Officer: You can stop that shit. You're in trouble. If you don't agree to stop pestering us, you'll vanish without trace.

Irina: No. I don't care how much I suffer.

Officer: Suffer! You don't know the meaning of the word.

Irina: Perhaps you're right. This is a nightmare, but we've suffered worse things, and it was real.

Officer: You're trying to tell me that only the Jews have suffered. If only we could get the dead back, they'd tell a tale or two. And most of them wouldn't be Jews. You're not human, though. If you were you wouldn't keep bothering us for such petty reasons.

Prisoner: Half our people perished. She's our Queen Esther!

Officer: Get back to reality.

Irina: You *are* reality – and you're human.

Officer: Yes, I think I am. But I have my job, that's all. Sometimes I think I'd rather kiss the Devil's arse than do it, but – you see my point?

Irina: I know: you have a wife, children I suppose, and a flat I'm sure, maybe a car, your own country to believe in and live for. You want your family to get the best out of life and enjoy it.

Officer: Of course I do. Don't you?

Irina: O yes! But for *all* my people, not only for myself.

Officer: Do you think people don't suffer where you want to go? Eh?

Irina: I'm sure they do, but at least they've chosen the country to suffer in, and the country to suffer for. On October 25th I went out of my house in the morning. On the street I heard steps behind me. Two men asked me to get into their car. 'I don't get into cars with strange men,' I said. 'Get out of my way.' One of them hit me, and I was dragged into the road. They behaved like gangsters. The car came up and they threw me in.

Officer: You're making it up. You're telling a story!

Irina: At police headquarters these thugs took me into a room and locked the door. I asked who they were, but they wouldn't say. They questioned me till evening. At night I was driven somewhere in a Black Maria. 'What am I accused of?' I asked. 'What have I done? Why are you treating me like this?' They pushed me into a room and began undressing me by force.

Officer: It's a pack of foul lies. Only women undress women. It's in the rules, and we never break the rules.

Irina: Their grubby hands touched my body. I'm thrown into a cell. My body, and my soul, go cold. I stay all night. There's a light bulb burning from the ceiling, and a large grated window. I take in every detail. But I'm terrified, so I lie on the bunk. My arms and back hurt. Only bread and water. They kept me fifteen days. I don't want to live in a world like this.

Officer: You asked for it. You'll get worse than that.

Irina: *You* knew all about it. You set them on to me. I recognised one of your bullies.

Prisoner: *(goes to help her)* She's ill, can't you see?

Officer: *(leaps to his feet, and slaps the Prisoner)* Leave her alone!

Irina: I'm not ill. I won't be.

Officer: You're a Soviet citizen, and nothing can alter that.

Irina: We're your guests, not your hostages. I want to go to Israel. Even if it takes my last breath I'll do it.

Officer: All right – I warned you. We've got a witness here who'll say he was part of your network, who helped you, who saw you, who saw others helping you and collecting the things you sent into camps. *(to Prisoner): Sign this.*

Prisoner: I won't.

Officer: What?

Prisoner: I can't.

Officer: Oh yes you will.

Prisoner: I won't.

Officer: He will. Don't let his brave face deceive you. I've seen them sell their wives, mothers, brothers, sisters for a spark of life. He will, no matter what he says now.

Irina: All right. Leave him alone. Maybe it would be

better for me in camp or prison. I'd at least know where I was. This is half life and half death. I try to live a normal life, but you won't let me. You send me to prison.

Officer: (*gets up and stands close to her, shouting*): *Just watch your step!*

Irina: I can't live in a sea of cunning. I'm a plain person. All I want is the basic freedom to go to Israel.

Officer: It means nothing to me – your mad craving. The only freedom here is for people who behave themselves – and who do as they're told. (*to Prisoner*) Sign here.

Prisoner: No.

Officer: Sign.

Prisoner stands and says nothing. The Officer sees that it is useless.

Officer: (*to Irina*) Get out.

Irina: You mean I can go?

Officer: Go on, get out. We've filled in your application form for a visa to leave the Soviet Union.

Irina Krichev begins to walk out. The Prisoner takes her arm. He quickly kisses her on the forehead.

Officer: Get back, you!

Irina: Thank you.

Exit Irina Krichev.

Short pause.

Officer: You play ball with us, and we'll play ball with you. You understood that, didn't you?

Prisoner: Yes.

Officer: Didn't you, you bastard?

Officer picks up the telephone, and dials two digits.

Officer: Hello? I'm returning the prisoner. I don't care how he gets back. I don't need him any more.

Officer puts the telephone down.

Officer: You can eat that good Russian mud all the way back to Mordovia. I hope it chokes you. You'll be hearing from us again.

Prisoner: Would *you* have done it?

Prisoner of Conscience walks to the door, which is opened by the Officer, and goes out. He is collected at the door and marched away.

Officer paces up and down, slowly, head lowered. He goes to the telephone and dials.

Officer: Hello? No, Comrade-General. Nothing. It was impossible. Nothing at all. Yes, sir, Kromy – 1922. When did I join the Party? 1943, sir, at the Front. Or 1944. No, it was 1943. That's right, sir. 1943. Yes, sir, the Great Patriotic War had already started. Certainly, sir. Lots of us *were* joining at that time.

Officer puts down the receiver. He takes out a cigarette. Then he stands still.

Officer: Nothing!

Officer throws the unlit cigarette violently across the room.

The telephone rings. Officer picks up the receiver.

Officer: All right: send them in.

CURTAIN on which is displayed the following:
Irina Krichev, whose real name is Ida Nudel, was sentenced in July 1978 to four years exile in Siberia.

PIT STRIKE

A television play

People

Joshua Reed
Jessie Reed
Marriot
Tom
Bullivant
Len
Percy
Petrol Station Manager
Petrol Station Attendant
Pam Seymour
Maria
Jerry (aged 5)
Barney (aged 8)
Matthew (aged 10)
Jack Seymour
Power Station Worker
Ron Williams
Police Inspector
Announcer (V.O.)

EXTRAS
Pickets
Police
Lorry Driver

PIT STRIKE

1. EXTERIOR. COALMINE. DAY.

The spinning headstocks of a coalmine in the Midlands are seen, a single unit against the sky, something on a human scale, almost like bicycle wheels.

2. EXTERIOR. POWER STATION. DAY.

The smoking chimney-tops of a power station show the architecture of pollution, the basic energy of technology, the initial raw processing of power towards modern life and comfort.

3. EXTERIOR. COALMINE. DAY.

The coalmine buildings.

Skipsheds, stores, canteen, pit baths.

On the other side are coal chutes and sidings.

4. EXTERIOR. DOCK GATES. DAY.

Riot outside Stopford dock gates in the south of England.

A line of colliers are pushing against the police who are trying to defend a lorry laden with coal.

The police are pushing back, and occasional violence on both sides is observed along the line.

5. EXTERIOR. COALMINE. DAY.

Colliers walking across the yard – as on a normal day at knocking-off time.

Joshua Reed is singled out among a group of friends. None is talking.

Joshua is six-feet-four in height, a burly man of about fifty years of age.

6. EXTERIOR. DOCK GATES (AS IN 4). DAY.

Ron: *(Welsh miner)* Get your false teeth into his knackers, Joshua!

Joshua is disturbed at such foul and unnecessary exhortation, and continues pushing.

7. EXTERIOR. A MINERS' HOUSING ESTATE SOMEWHERE IN THE MIDLANDS. DAY.

An occasional car by the kerb.

A child passes on a bicycle.

A young long-haired collier walks by with a dog.

The weather is cold.

Joshua is seen in his front garden tapping the frosty earth with a spade. It is not possible to dig.

8. INTERIOR. THE REEDS' LIVING ROOM. EVENING.

A settee, lining a wall, obliquely faces a television set.

There is a table under the window, with plain chairs on three sides of it.

On the opposite wall, by the door opening into the hall, is a tall glass-fronted cupboard for pots and less perishable foods.

A coal fire is burning in the grate. By the side of the fire an electric kettle is plugged in.

On the shelf is a framed photograph of two young men – their sons.

Jessie Reed (Joshua's wife), a tall, thin, brown-faced woman, sits on the settee knitting at an almost finished jumper.

Joshua is placed by the table under the window rolling cigarettes.

There is a small black leatherbound Bible resting casually on the other side of the table.

The television set is in black and white, and the news is on.

Announcer: '. . . with thousands more miners idle in the Midlands, the stoppage seems to be complete.'
Joshua: Idle! Couldn't they just say 'on strike'? Why does it have to be 'idle'?
Jessie: It ain't his fault.
Joshua: He's saying it, though.
Jessie: He's been told to.

Joshua puts five rolled cigarettes into his tin.

Joshua: It's wickedness to be idle. (*looking at TV announcer*) Graven image come to life.

Switches off the television set.

Joshua: The truth means nothing to them. None of us want to be idle.

Jessie puts down her knitting and flicks on the electric kettle.

Jessie: I got a piece of nice brisket for tomorrow's dinner.
Joshua: *(lights a cigarette)* How much was it?

Jessie goes across to the cupboard.

Jessie: Ten bob.
Joshua: We've got to watch the money.

Jessie brings cups and saucers, sugar and milk to the table.

Jessie: If we get skint, they'll let us have things on tick at shop.
Joshua: What if we lose, I wonder?
Jessie: Some people say the country won't need coal much longer.
Joshua: We'll see.

Joshua stands up to put some coal on the fire.

Joshua: They think they've got us where they want us, Jessie. This strike's the last thing *I* wanted. Same with the young blokes. They've got most to lose. I'm glad our two lads got out of it. They're better off living in Leicester, I know that much.
Jessie: Don't get upset, Josh.
Joshua: I know. But time's the most valuable thing in the world. We've only got three score years and ten.
Jessie: If we're lucky. We've had worse bouts, though.

Kettle whistles.

128

Joshua: For better causes. Satan makes work for idle hands. I don't like it.

Jessie pours water into the teapot.

Jessie: Well, we weren't too bad off after the war, were we? It was when they started closing pits that trouble started.

Pours tea, puts milk and sugar in it, and stirs it up for him.

Jessie: Come on, I know you allus get thirsty when you get downhearted.
Joshua: *(lightly)* Aye – worry does dry you up, don't it, duck? Thought there was oil enough to drink.
Jessie: They didn't know coal was the stuff of life, as well as bread.
Joshua: *(reaches for his Bible)* It's unnatural – not being at work. When my muscles don't ache at the end of the day, I feel as if the wind'll take me off when I'm out on the street. I'm not used to it. *(a sudden lighter mood)* Well, I'll have more time to read!
Jessie: *(resumes her knitting)* You can practise more with the football team, as well.
Joshua: One day we'll reach the Promised Land, though. Be a feast in Shiloh, that will, Jessie, my love.
Jessie: But somebody'll still have to dig the coal out, and pay for it.
Joshua: Allus was like that, and allus will be. *(laughs)* As long as we get some of the milk and honey!

9. INTERIOR. ROOM AT THE MINERS' WELFARE CLUB. NIGHT.

Joshua and Marriot are at a table playing draughts, with Tom as an onlooker.

Marriot is a darkish man of forty-five – medium height, a person of know-all aspect, and of volatile mood.

Tom is a man of thirty, tall and thin, and somewhat sombre in character.

Marriot moves a king-piece on the draughtboard.

Marriot: There's not even picketing to do. Every pit and power station in Trent Valley buttoned-up solid.

Tom: George next door to me's never had a cold in his life before. Up to his waist in water, week after week, and he's as chirpy as a bird. But as soon as the strike starts, he gets a banger – 'flu, in fact. He'll get over it when that hooter goes again, I told his missis, don't you worry.

Marriot: I'm doing up the kitchen. Had the paper and paste for two years in a cupboard under the stairs. Be done tomorrow, though.

Joshua holding half a pint, which is like a thimble in his big hand.

Joshua: I'm patching the old bike shed up.

He watches the draughtboard astutely and makes a move.

Tom: That took you long enough. You'll be at it next week, the way you're going.

Joshua: I'm doing some reading as well.

Marriot: What does the Good Book say? Will we win?

Joshua: 'The Lord is our rock, and our fortress, and our deliverer. He is our shield and our salvation.' It's not for us to say whether we'll win or not. 'Through the brightness before Him were coals of fire kindled.'

Tom: You want to get a proper book, Josh. Read Karl Marx, and join the Party.

Joshua: I believe in God.

Laughter: Joshua moves draught piece.

Marriot: Go on! Ever seen him?
Joshua: No, but I reckon He's down the pit often enough. He giveth life, and He taketh it away. You can't tell me otherwise.

During these remarks he has leapfrogged four kings of Marriot's from the board.

Enter Bullivant, union official.

Marriot at the draughts game being ended.

Marriot: Bloody 'ell! Now what are we going to do for the rest of the evening?
Bullivant: You can get off home and pack your kitbags. There's blokes wanted to go south tomorrow. Got no colliers in London, so they need reinforcements to bottle up power stations there as well. You'll be helping the Kent blokes – that's what you'll be doing.
Marriot: Bang goes the rest of the paper hanging. The missis wain't be pleased about this, Bullivant.
Bullivant: Well she'll have to be, won't she.
Tom: Is your car in good nick?
Marriot: A1. Been servicing it ever since we came out.
Joshua: I'll go.
Tom: That's good. We can all chip in for petrol.
Bullivant: You'll get an allowance for that.
Marriot: We'll take the good fight right into Caesar's camp, Josh! He's bloody strong down there.
Joshua: I've never been to London.
Tom: Now's your chance, then. Tea next week at Buckingham Palace.
Bullivant: Yer – wined and dined at the Bloody Tower! Come with me, Marriot, and I'll tell you your billeting arrangements. All official. You'll have the time of your life at Dirty Dick's, if I know you.

10. INTERIOR. JESSIE REED'S KITCHEN. NEXT MORNING.

Breakfast has been eaten.

Jessie is putting a shirt and underwear into an overnight case.

Jessie: Did they say how long you'll be gone?

Joshua putting on his overcoat and cap. A car horn sounds from outside.

Joshua: That's 'em. Don't know. Maybe a week.
Jessie: Look after yourself.
Joshua: We take care of each other, my love. It's all for one and one for all down the pit – *and* on top. I'll send you a picture postcard.

They embrace and kiss.

Jessie: I'd die if owt 'appened to you.
Joshua: *(laughs)* I've worked down the pit for thirty-five years, and nowt's happened, thank the Lord, so it's not likely to in any place down south.

Joshua goes to the door. The horn sounds again – for the third time.

Joshua leaps back, snatches his Bible from the top of the dresser, and is stuffing it in his back pocket as he goes out.

Jessie runs after him and throws a scarf around his neck.

11. INTERIOR. MARRIOT'S BIG OLD BANGER. GOING SOUTH. DAY.

There are stickers on the back and sides of the car saying 'Support the miners'.

*In the car are five colliers: Joshua, Len and Percy in the back;
Tom and Marriot in the front.*

Percy: *(young collier)* Let's go down the motorway. Be
  there in three hours.
Marriot: Caffs are cheaper on the Great North Road.
Len: You aren't frightened o' them posh places, are you?
Percy: Thinks they'll skin him alive!

Laughter.

Marriot: I'll bloody get you there.

*Joshua [commentary] his eyes fixed on the well-appointed
cottages and gentle landscape along the route.*

Joshua: Not like where I was born. God's wonders and
  beauties dwell a bit more here. He brought us out of the
  house of bondage, though I often think we're still in it. I
  don't suppose going down here will change things
  much. Should have stayed at home.
Marriot: Cheer up, Joshua. We're going to win this time.
Tom: Heath'll be playing his organ by candlelight before
  we've done!
Marriot: As long as we get to the next petrol station
  before we run out of juice.

12. EXTERIOR. PETROL STATION. DAY.

Miners' car draws into the forecourt.

*All five get out quickly. They meet frosty air, waft arms, and
get legs going up and down to shift the stiffness out of
themselves.*

Joshua, feeling the discomfort of the protruding Bible at his back pocket, takes it out and holds it – unobtrusively – in his hand.

Attendant, a youth of twenty, comes across to serve them.

The Manager, a little red-faced man with moustache, comes out of his office.

Marriot: Put six gallons in the tank, duck.

The Manager, walking to the pump, has to pass the back of the car. He sees 'Support the miners' stickers, and glares with indignation.

He takes the nozzle from the Attendant, and almost slings it back in its slot.

Manager: Don't serve 'em.
Attendant: Why?
Manager: You heard.
Attendant: I don't get it.
Manager: Not a drop.
Marriot: What's the bloody game?

They gather around the Manager at the garage door.

Manager: Clear off to some other place!
Joshua: Ain't he got none left?
Manager: You won't get any petrol here.

Joshua still not quite taking in the situation.

Joshua: How far's the next garage?
Manager: That's your problem. You ought to be driven back to work.
Joshua: Oh, it's like that, is it?
Manager: Yes, it *is*. I do eighty hours a week, and don't get the wages you lot make. I started work at fourteen,

and I've never stopped going since. Nobody would give a damn if I went on strike.

Len: I don't suppose you've ever been more than a stone's throw from daylight. I'd like to see you do a week down the pit.

Percy: Made his bloody pile, I expect.

Manager swinging back at them courageously.

Manager: If it were my job I'd do it. *And* I wouldn't moan and go on strike about it.

Joshua, in a strange situation, like a fish out of water, reverts to his old source of solace and comfort – the Bible – in order, as he thinks, to get out of the fix with dignity. He pushes his mates aside.

Marriot: Steady on, Joshua.

Joshua advances on the Manager, who looks at him.

In this scene Joshua can go with alarming suddenness (and subtlety) from the flippant to the deeply serious, half-fanatical reality. He is moved, it would seem, by something outside of himself.

Joshua: Nay, lad, I may be six cubits and a span in height . . .

Len: What's that in metric, Josh?

Joshua: . . . but I'll not touch a hair of thy idolater's head. Pharaoh is pursuing us, and we need food for our chariot. Don't we, lads? *(before they can respond)* 'And Moses said unto the people, Remember this day, in which ye came out of Egypt, *(brandishing his Bible)* out of the house of bondage; for by strength of hand the Lord brought you out from this place.'

Len: You tell the bastard, Josh.

Marriot: And if he won't listen, throw the bloody book at him.

Manager: You won't be served here.

Joshua: (*turning on Marriot*) Don't insult the Book. It's the Lord's word. All His statutes are in it, and I won't throw the Book at him lest it fall into the mud of iniquity, and be trodden under-foot by slothful worshippers of the graven image.

The manager takes this opportunity of Joshua's deflected rage [or whatever it is] to get out of the situation with as little loss of face as possible.

Manager: All right – you can have your petrol. Then be on your way. I don't want you on my premises.

Marriot: (*turning to the others*) So what was all that about, then?

Manager: (*to Attendant*) Get going! What are you standing there for?

Manager goes back into his office.

Attendant, happy at the outcome, slots in the nozzle.

Marriot – gets out his wallet to pay.

Joshua – is happier now, after their adventure, which has made the break from home more decisive. He watches the petrol pouring in.

Joshua: Milk and golden honey!

Len: Come on, I'm bloody freezing.

Joshua: Pay up, and let's get on to them power stations.

Marriot: (*paying Attendant*) You'll be pumping it in by hand next week.

13. INTERIOR. CAR GOING INTO LONDON. DAY.

Marriot: Keep your eyes pasted on them maps.

Percy with maps unopened on his knee.

Percy: I'll get you there.
Len: Came last year with his wife, didn't you, Percy?
Percy: Ay. Just keep going straight on.

Marriot overtakes a bus.

The driver gives the thumbs-up sign.

14. EXTERIOR. CAR. LONDON BRIDGE. DAY.

The car crosses the Thames on London Bridge.

View of Tower Bridge to the left.

15. INTERIOR. CAR. LONDON BRIDGE. DAY.

Marriot: You've only seen this on telly, Joshua, ain't you?
Joshua: Aye. And it looked better there.
Tom: Where do you go on holiday, then?
Joshua: Bridlington. Not every year, either.

As they are going over the actual river, Joshua's voice makes the following commentary.

At the latter part of it, the Bankside Power Station is seen to the right.

(*off*) 'We will pass over armed before the Lord into the Land of Canaan, that the possession of our inheritance on this side Jordan may be ours.'

16. EXTERIOR. A STREET IN THE BLACKHEATH-GREENWICH AREA. DAY.

The miners' car draws up at a large sedate house.

Marriot getting out on to the pavement and pulling Joshua's overnight case out of the car boot.

Marriot: Number twenty-eight. Them's your digs, Joshua. Just ring the bell and ask for Mrs Seymour.
Joshua: Mrs who?
Marriot: Seymour. Go on. She won't bite you.

Joshua getting awkwardly out of the car.

Joshua: When shall I see you lot?
Marriot: (*getting back at the wheel*) We'll meet after – in the nearest boozer.
Joshua: Where's that, then?
Marriot: Down the street and across the road. You'll see it.

Joshua looks at the car, which drives away at speed.

Joshua looks up and down the strange road.

A man in 'city' garb comes by, and glances at him.

Joshua wonders whether he shouldn't get straight back to Nottinghamshire.

But after this hesitation he opens the gate and walks along the path to the door, which opens just as his hand moves towards the bell.

Pam Seymour is facing him.

She is a 35 year old university lecturer, small and fair.

Pam: Oh!
Joshua: I'm down from Notts because of the strike. Joshua Reed.
Pam: *(laughs)* You're our coalminer? Come in. I was just going to the shops, but it can wait.
Joshua: I suppose I *am* a bit of a shock!
Pam: No, no. We said we'd put one of you up. There's no shortage of accommodation. Everyone's rallying around splendidly.

17. INTERIOR. SEYMOUR'S HOUSE. DAY.

Joshua follows Pam into the hall.

Pam: Put your case there, and come into the kitchen. You must be tired.
Joshua: I'm all right.

The house is well-furnished – Heal's style – not opulent, though it's totally strange to Joshua.

He appears diffident, however, rather than out of place.

The living-room, dining-room, kitchen are one big area, about three times the size of the groundfloor of his own house.

The Wellington boots on his feet are muddy from travel, and he hesitates at the threshold.

Pam: Don't mind about that. The *au pair* will be cleaning up tomorrow.

Joshua: *(going in)* It's good of you to put me up.

Pam: Oh, we're all behind you in your fight. Jack and I have been socialists for a long time. Maria!

Maria: *(the au pair)* Si, señora?

Pam: Quieres enseñar el señor a su cuarto, que ya esta preparado desde ayer?

Maria: Si, señora.

Joshua: You're very clever to speak a foreign language like that.

Pam: *(laughs)* It's only pidgin Spanish. Learned it on holiday. I'm glad the miners are going to teach this government a lesson. The sooner power is where it should be, the better. If you'll take your case and follow Maria she'll show you to your room. Then you can come down and we'll have some tea.

Joshua follows Maria to a small room at the back of the house.

17A. INTERIOR. BEDROOM. DAY.

Maria: Here it is.

Joshua: You do speak English, then?

Maria: Of course.

Joshua: I thought you did.

Maria: I'm a student.

Joshua: That's nice!

Maria leaves.

The room has a wardrobe, a single bed, a writing table, and a scalding radiator – which Joshua touches so that his hand jumps back from it.

He closes the slightly open windows, then takes the Bible from his back packet and puts it on the table.

He takes off his jacket, hangs it on the bed, and washes his hands at the sink.

Then he goes downstairs.

Joshua enters kitchen area.

17B. INTERIOR. KITCHEN. DAY.

Pam: Everything okay?

Joshua: First class!

Pam: There's always food in the kitchen. When you feel hungry just help yourself. Sugar?

Joshua: Three.

Pam: We know you'll win your fight. Jack will drive you to the power station in the morning before he goes to work. He teaches at university, like me, but I only go in twice a week. You'll get there in time for your picketing. Biscuit?

Joshua: *(takes one hesitantly)* I can find it on the bus. Or my mates'll pick me up.

Pam: No, we're glad to help. We have *two* cars, so you'll be taken there. We can't do enough for you, really. What town are you from?

Joshua: Ashfield. The end of the world, some people call it. Wind comes at it five ways, all year round.

Pam: What are conditions like?

Joshua suspects that since he has run Ashfield down a bit too much to this stranger, she wants him to run it down a bit more, for him to complain, in fact.

And his pride won't let him do this.

Joshua: In't pit?

Pam: No. I know *they're* horrible.

Joshua: Got to be. But most people think we're bred to it and don't mind it. Every day you go down it's like going down the very first day. But you do sort of get used to it.

Pam: I mean *housing* conditions.

Joshua: *(takes another biscuit)* I don't complain. It's a good enough place – bit o' garden back and front.

Pam: Oh! *(she's at a loss for words)* Do you have any children, Joshua?

Joshua: Two lads – married. Live forty miles away. I felt young again when they left home, though. I suppose when grandchildren start coming to see me it'll put the years on me tenfold.

Pam: Do you think so?

Joshua: Oh, I shan't mind. It's the grandad as teaches kids, isn't it? Same as my grandad taught me a thing or two. That's life, I allus say.

Pam: Must be strange, living all your life in one place.

Joshua: *(not committing himself)* It's all right. *(pause)* Was you born here?

Pam: No. My father was a vicar in the West Country.

Joshua: Was he? Read his Bible, eh?

Pam: *(laughs at his joke)* Sometimes!

Joshua: Once a week, like?

Pam not wanting to discuss her father.

Pam: I've forgotten your towels, and Maria's gone.

Joshua: My wife put one in for me, so don't bother.

Pam: I'll pop up with them myself.

Joshua pours more tea. Pam goes upstairs and into Joshua's room.

17C. INTERIOR. BEDROOM. DAY.

Pam enters room and puts the towel on the radiator. She sees the Bible on the table. She opens it idly, letting the pages drift back into position. She raises her eyebrows in surprise. There is a shattering noise of children coming from downstairs.

17D. INTERIOR. KITCHEN. DAY.

Jerry aged five, Barney aged eight, Matthew aged ten, rush into the kitchen, and stand still on seeing Joshua.

Joshua: Hello, then.
Jerry: Are you our coal-minder?
Matthew: Miner!
Pam: His name is Joshua. And we're helping him in his strike. Joshua, this is Barney. And that's Jerry.
Matthew: And I'm Matthew.
Barney: (*screeching*) Horrid Jasper Clewes at school was boasting that they had two miners at their house, but now I can say ya-ya-ya we have a miner as well!
Pam: (*obviously pleased*) Now do stop it. Go and wash your hands, then you can have your tea.

18. EXTERIOR. STREET. DUSK.

Joshua wearing overcoat, Wellingtons, and cap, walking up the street. Some people pass, strangers in every way. Even the subdued street lighting is different. Joshua stands at the kerb of the A2 main road, with rush-hour traffic streaming out of London.

Lighting is dimmer than the usual glare because of power cuts. He is bemused, rather than bewildered, and watches the traffic, intending to cross.

Joshua crosses immediately when one lorry has passed, so that he touches the back of it, and there is enough safe space before the one following can get to him.

It is successful, neatly timed, and dangerous.

19. INTERIOR. PUBLIC HOUSE. EVENING.

Lit up public house. Joshua enters. The place is fairly full. Marriot, Tom and Percy sit at a table and Joshua walks over to them. The others have taken off their overcoats and caps, but Joshua stays buttoned-up while he is there.

Joshua: I knew I'd find yo' lot in a place like this.
Marriot: You must have smelled your way.
Percy: We thought you couldn't tear yourself away from that cushy billet. Pint, is it?
Joshua: (*nods*) Where's the others?

Percy goes up to the bar for more drinks.

Marriot: Gone to't pictures. Sex film on.
Joshua: What's *your* digs like?
Marriot: As posh as they come. Real solidarity. Me and Tom's sharing a room. Do you snore, Tom?
Tom: What the 'ell does it matter? You ain't going to marry me.
Percy: (*putting drinks down*) Not on the wages you get, he's not.
Tom: Ne' mind. I'll have a raise soon!
Percy: So we've been led to believe.
Marriot: She nice, your landlady, Josh?
Joshua: Very amiable. She's got some good kids. I ain't met the husband yet.
Percy: Maybe you wain't.

144

Joshua: Don't be so daft. What's the programme for tomorrow?
Marriot: Sit down, and I'll tell yer.

20. INTERIOR. SEYMOUR'S KITCHEN. NEXT MORNING.

Jack Seymour, wearing a garish Russian-style shirt, cooking egg and bacon at the stove.

Pam is sitting at the table, smoking.

Jack: I can hear him already.
Pam: The children took to him immediately.
Jack: Trying to make me jealous?
Pam: I saw a Bible in his room when I took the towels up.
Jack: A Bible?
Pam: Well?
Jack: A Bible!
Pam: Here he comes.
Jack: With the children.

Enter Joshua. He has Jerry on his shoulder, and is holding Barney's hand.

And his Wellingtons are held in his teeth. He is followed closely by Matthew.

Jack: Good morning.
Joshua: *(puts Jerry down)* Good morning.
Pam: I hope you slept well. Eggs and bacon? My husband, Jack.
Joshua: Like a top. *(he shakes hands with Jack)* Pleased to meet you.
Jack: Glad to have you with us.

Joshua: *(to Pam)* Yes, please. Funny how hungry I feel in London. *(to Barney)* I could eat a horse between two mattresses!

Pam: We'll give you something better than that.

Joshua: But not tastier! *(sits down, and puts the Wellington boots by his feet)* Have you got a few newspapers I could have?

Pam: *(puzzled)* Certainly.

Joshua: Old 'uns, not new 'uns!

Pam: Matthew, get Joshua some from under the sink.

Both Jerry and Barney rush to do it.

Jerry: I'll get 'em.

Barney: He asked *me*.

Jerry: No, he didn't.

Barney: Yes, he did.

They both bring some.

Joshua folds the newspapers meticulously around his legs below the knees, much as a soldier in 1914 would put on his puttees.

Joshua then pulls his Wellingtons up and on over them.

Joshua: *(looking at Barney)* That's if I should get into a scrimmage, and somebody wants to play a game of kick shins with me.

Jack: *(puffing at his pipe)* Who are you expecting kicks from?

Pam filling a briefcase with pamphlets and papers.

Pam: As if you couldn't guess!

Joshua: It's not what you expect. It's what you *might* get. Not that I like that sort of thing.

Matthew: They put newspapers there, in case the police kick them. That's what we talk about at school.

146

Joshua: *(eating his breakfast)* You're a good learner.
Barney: Can *I* kick you?
Pam: Barney!
Joshua: As a sort of test?
Jack: *(pouring more tea)* That's no way to treat a guest. *(to Joshua)* We have to bring them up on the right side.
Barney: *(pleading)* Let me try, Joshua.
Joshua: Have a go, then. And if I feel it, I'll give you a penny.
Barney: Can I really?
Joshua: If you like.
Pam: Oh no!
Joshua: He'll be all right. Go on. Ready, set, *Go!*

Barney runs from the other side of the room. His shoes strike Joshua's Wellingtons, and he falls back, slightly hurt.

Barney: *Oh,* Blast!
Jack: Let that be a lesson to you.
Joshua: *(pulls Barney close)* See what a brave lad you've got? Here's a shilling. Only don't do it every day, will yer? Now you can tell your smarmy school pals that you've got a collier in your house as well.

21. EXTERIOR. POWER STATION GATES. DAY.

Things are quiet. Pickets stand around in groups.

A police car is parked.

The pickets have a couple of cars farther up the road.

Joshua leans against the railing, well wrapped up, reading his Bible.

Marriot sits on the kerb engrossed in a newspaper.

Len is beating his arms across his chest to keep out the cold.

Len: At least it was warm down pit.
Tom: How long before they crack, I wonder?
Marriot: It'll come very sudden, mark my word.
Percy: We've bin here a week already.
Marriot: *(to Joshua)* Can you dig up a prophecy for us out of your Bible, Joshua?
Joshua: *(moodily)* It ain't that sort of book. We've got to endure, and not go whoring after strange gods. That's all I know.
Marriot: A lot of good that is. *(sees Worker coming out of the power station gates)* Let's see what *he* knows. Hey, mate, what's happening in there?
Worker: You're doing all right.
Percy: How much coal's left?
Worker: They're shovelling the dust in now. By tomorrow they won't have enough to light a five-watt bulb.

Worker goes off.

Marriot: About bloody time.
Bullivant: *(very important-looking with clipboard)* We want one car and six men from you lot.
Marriot: What's up now?
Bullivant: Get on the dual carriageway, and head for Stopford Docks. They're trying to get coal out of the gates and the police are giving the lads hell. There'll be 30 cars altogether with six in a car, and ten motorbikes. You're part of the Flying Picket. Come on, lads, *move!*

Joshua, Percy, Tom, Marriot, Denis, Len gather together.

Percy: Where are the other cars? We don't want to get there and find nobody elsc.

Bullivant: You'd argue the hind leg off a donkey. They're on their way. Some from headquarters, some from Greenwich, most from Kent, and some from my grandma's back passage. Now for Christ's sake get going. I'll get a bloody ulcer before this lot's over.
Joshua: *(slots Bible back into his pocket)* Let's be off, then.
Tom: Bloody sergeant-major.

They run to the car.

Bullivant: I'll be down there before you, don't you worry.

22. EXTERIOR. DUAL CARRIAGEWAY AND MOTORWAY. DAY.

A dozen or so cars, miners' stickers in all of them, are speeding along the road, overtaking when they can.

Inside Marriot's car. Marriot's face is deadset, as he tries to keep up speed yet stay safe on the strange highway.

Everyone inside is tense.

Len: Here come the Flying Pickets.
Percy: Next time we'll have aeroplanes.
Tom: Bloody tanks, you mean.
Marriot: As far as I'm concerned we ought to hire taxis.
Len: You'll have to file an application in spifflicate for that.

23. EXTERIOR. DOCK GATES. DAY.

Cars are drawing up to the kerb and doors already opening as men in the colliers' uniform of overcoats and caps and Wellingtons leap out.

149

Police vans and cars are around the site. A line of police are trying to force a crowd of pickets back against the pavement, and a lorry by the open dock gates is waiting for clearance.

Reinforcements spread along the thin line of the pickets already there.

Joshua rushes up with the rest of them and begins to push. Ron Williams, a Welshman, is next to him.

The sudden reinforcement has thrown the police off balance, and they begin to go back, and therefore to get more vicious.

Ron: *(to Joshua)* Thought you'd never get here. Push, for God's sake. The swivel-eyed bleeders have been thumping the guts out of us all morning.
Joshua: My name's Joshua.

Policeman kicks Joshua, and reels back from the padded Wellington.

Joshua turns side-on and pushes.

Ron: *(shouts)* Go on, then, Joshua, get your false teeth into his knackers!
Police Inspector: If I get hold of you, you Welsh Baptist bastard, I'll knock *your* false teeth down your throat.
Ron: *(stunned)* What? What?

Ron gets the Police Inspector in a half-nelson.

The Police Inspector's hat and Ron's cap go flying. Constables pull the Officer clear, and colliers drag Ron off — a very ugly moment.

The colliers, however, push forward, too close to the lorry for its driver to think of getting clear of the docks. It has become a stalemate.

Police Inspector, cap back on, smiling, goes to a police van by the kerb and talks to other officers.

Ron: I'll kill him.

Joshua: *(handing Ron his cap)* You won't. Vengeance is mine, saith the Lord. It was only in the heat of the moment.

Ron: *(putting cap on)* But one more crack like that and I'll get him – if I have to serve five years!

Police Inspector goes from police van to lorry and speaks to the driver. He motions him back inside the dock gates. Lorry reverses in, and the gates are closed.

Cheers from the pickets.

Marriot: Looks like a goal.

Joshua: For the moment.

Bullivant talking to the Police Inspector. Comes over to the men.

Bullivant: They won't open the gates again till the strike's over. We might as well go home – so they reckon. We've won this round, anyway.

Marriot: *(sitting on the kerb)* Spin me another.

Bullivant: I know. Stay there till I find what we're to do.

Marriot: It's a struggle, Josh, every bit of the way.

Len: It ain't over yet, not by a long fart.

Joshua: We'll see what the Union says. I don't like this. Expect we'll laugh at it one day, but it's bad for life and limb, this is. The Lord's got nowt to do we' this. Satan, more like.

Percy: We're only fighting for our rights.

Joshua, troubled at the fighting, getting his Bible – to check that it's still there.

Joshua: Aye – I know.

A sudden juddering roar of voices, as if the fighting is going to start again. It is only the police canteen opening its shutter, to the colliers' applause.

Marriot: *(sounding more cheerful)* Give us the Sermon on the Mount, Joshua.
Joshua: I don't read that. I stop at the Prophets.
Marriot: I expect we'll be going back to Greenwich soon, anyhow.
Tom: *(pointing across the road)* Just look at that, will yer——

Policemen are standing around the canteen van drinking tea, and a few colliers have joined them, and are also drinking from paper cups.

Marriot: Boggers 'ud scrounge milk out of a virgin's tit.

He is almost envious of them.

Joshua: I suppose some of the police have got soft hearts as well. They're only like us, if you tek that false raiment off their backs.
Tom: Bloody scroungers, though, all the same.

Marriot, ruminating at the back of the crowd, sees an enormous high-sided lorry laden with coal leaving the docks by a concealed gate farther down the road.

Marriot: Josh! Hey, Taffy, look at that! Don't mek a fuss, but follow me.

Marriot, Joshua, Ron, Tom and Percy move quickly to the nearest car.

Ron: Jump in. We'll get him.

24. INTERIOR. CAR. DAY.

Joshua sits next to Ron, who is driving.

They set off after the rogue-lorry.

Marriot: Some blokes 'ud sell their soul for a barrel o' beer and a kipper.

Percy: Maybe he's only doing it for a cup of tea, the stupid sod.

Tom: He pulled a bloody fast one, whatever he's getting.

Percy: There ain't much we can do, even if we do catch it up.

Joshua, peering ahead through the traffic.

Joshua: Just keep at him.

Uncomfortable from the Bible in his back pocket.

Tom: Should a left that Bible in your digs, Josh.

Joshua: I will next time.

Marriot: He's turned off somewhere.

Joshua: That's more than he dare do.

Ron: Corner him like a rat if he does.

Joshua: He'll keep straight on, you see.

Ron overtaking a bus.

Ron: He won't get it into a power station. The lads'll be waiting everywhere. Sink their boots into the likes of him.

Joshua: They'll have a secret gate for him to get into. We've got to stop him on the way.

Marriot: I don't bloody see how we'll do that.

The lorry is going slowly up a slip road leading to a motorway, and the miners' car is close behind.

Ron: I hope he don't start rolling back.

Joshua: Just keep close.

Marriot: Not too close, or it'll be the end of my promising career.

Near-hysterical laughter from all except Joshua.

Joshua: When I was a youth I used to get at the back of a lorry like that on my bike, and have a free pull all the way up a hill. When I was even younger we used to run after it and just jump on.

The tension builds up in the car which is only a few feet from the lorry's towering back.

It is drizzling, and Ron flicks on the windscreen wipers.

Tom: We're so close, he don't know we're here.

Marriot: He'll get a fat bonus, though –

Percy: He'll need compo before we've done wi' 'im'.

Marriot: – right up his arse.

Joshua: How fast would you say he's going?

Ron: Same as us. About ten miles per hour.

Joshua: Will he slow down up that hill?

Ron: Bound to.

Joshua looks hard at the lorry-back, and weighs his chances.

Joshua: I know what to do.

Marriot: It ain't a game o' football, Josh.

Joshua opening the car door.

Joshua: I know. Keep a bit back from the lorry, there's a good lad.

Percy: For God's sake, Joshua.

Joshua: I'll be all right – as long as the Lord stays with me. Keep just a little bit behind, though. I don't want my guts crushing in.

Marriot: You're taking chances, Josh.

25. EXTERIOR. MOTORWAY SLIP ROAD. DAY.

Joshua gets out of the car, closes the door carefully and quietly, then runs in an exaggerated fashion, keeping up with the lorry.

When he catches up with it, his outward palms touch the lorry back as if giving it a push.

Joshua turns to look at his worried mates through the windscreen.

Joshua gets to work to loosen the steel pins at the back of the lorry.

Black spray is coming up from the wheels.

Joshua is continually wiping it away, working with a permanent squint, struggling to loosen the great bar.

He is terrified, but works on, much as he might when underground and sensing danger. A hand flaps behind to check that his Bible is still there.

It is. Joshua smiles. With renewed vigour, he works while running.

The bar is half-way out.

Joshua: *(voice only)* And the Lord said – see, I have given into thine hand Jericho – shout; for the Lord hath given you the city – that the wall fell down flat – that the wall fell down flat – the wall fell –

A gap appears in the bottom of the tailgate, and cobbles of coal begin to fall.

But he works till the rest of the bar is free.

The tailgate flaps ominously.

Joshua leaps clear.

The car slows to avoid the avalanche.

Joshua runs back to it and leaps – not without difficulty – into the door held open.

A hand extends from the back to give him a pull.

Avalanche of coal.

The car gets by, just in time.

The lorry does not stop for a while, not realising what has happened, so that the whole of its load, to the last cobble, is shed along the road.

26. INTERIOR. CAR. DAY.

Inside car: hysterical laughter.

Joshua is deathly pale.

Ron: Shake my hand, Joshua. I've never seen anything like it.
Joshua: *(shaking the hand quickly)* Keep your eyes on the road.
Marriot: Wait till I tell the others.
Joshua: Say nowt. Just thank the Lord. *(Joshua feels at his back pocket, and his face registers the fact that he has lost something)* My Bible's gone.

26A. EXTERIOR. DAY.

Cut to the mountain of the coal in the road.

A police car is stationed at either end.

26B. INTERIOR. DAY. CAR.

Joshua: My Bible.
Marriot: It must be under that load o' coal, Joshua.
Joshua: I bought it for a tanner in Worksop market one
Saturday night when I was fourteen. It was on a stall
among a lot o' rammel. I just grabbed it and paid for
it——

Joshua closes his eyes, as if going to sleep.

27. INTERIOR. KITCHEN AT THE SEYMOURS. DAY.

*Joshua is dressed to leave, to go back north, his small
overnight case and two plastic carrier bags by the table.*

Pam: Well, Joshua, are you glad it's over?
Joshua: (*nods*) I want to get back and start ripping that
coal out again. They had to give in, though, didn't
they?

*Pam, putting salt and bread on the table, setting knife and
fork.*

Pam: With so many soldiers in Ulster they could hardly
afford to fight the miners as well.

Joshua: I suppose you might put it like that. We just wanted a reasonable wage, that's all.

Pam: Don't the workers want a bigger say in how the country's run?

Joshua: It's the first I've heard of it. We can beat Caesar any time, though, and that's a fact.

Pam: *(setting a meal before him)* We'll be sorry to see you go.

Joshua: We all must.

Pam: Are they your things?

Joshua: Them's 'em.

Pam: I hear you lost your Bible in a scrimmage.

Joshua: I'll get another.

Pam: You were a bit of a hero, they say.

Joshua: The Lord protected me. I've learned a lot during this strike. I suppose you're never too old to learn.

Pam: *(looks at him, and wonders)* True.

Joshua: I'll be glad to see my wife again and be back at work. It's where I belong. I hate being down there in the dark, but I like it as well. You're on your own, stuck in a three-foot seam they can't get the machines into. Half a mile down and two along. But I remember all the bits from the Bible while I am working. I shan't forget the different chaps I've met from all over the country. It's marvellous how we've stuck together in this trouble. It's a wonder I'm alive, though, after getting the back off that coal lorry. *(laughs)* It went all over the road. Terrible waste. But I expect they scooped it up and took it somewhere!

Pam: The children cried last night when they heard you'd be leaving. I hope you'll come and see us whenever you're in London.

Joshua: I can't say when that'll be.

Pam: You never know. Look, I've a suitcase upstairs we don't need. I'll pack these carrier bags in it.

Joshua: It's all right. I'll manage.

Pam: You can use it when you go on your travels.

Before he can say anything she goes upstairs with his carrier-bags.

28. INTERIOR. HALL/STAIRS. DAY.

In the hall she takes a Bible, similar to the one Joshua lost, out of the bookcase – to put it into the case for him. The Bible belonged to her father.

Noise of motor horn sounding from Marriot's car waiting outside the house.

29. INTERIOR/EXTERIOR. MARRIOT'S CAR CROSSING LONDON BRIDGE. DAY.

'Support the Miners' stickers still on it.

Backshot of power station fully working.

Joshua: *(voice only)* 'Wherefore have I seen them dismayed and turned away back? And their mighty ones are beaten down, and are fled apace, and look not back . . .'
Marriot: Cheer up, Joshua. We'll be home soon.
Joshua: I'll be a happy man then, I can tell you!

30. EXTERIOR. GREEN FIELDS. DAY.

Joshua's P.O.V. from car.

31. EXTERIOR. MINING TOWN. DAY.

Joshua's P.O.V. from car.

32. EXTERIOR. COLLIERY. DAY.

Miners going to work.

FADE OUT